Great Britain

Switzerland

Germany

Sweden

Denmark

URBAN SCHOOLS IN EUROPE

A STUDY TOUR OF FIVE CITIES

BY:

JOHN W. McLEOD   F.A.I.A.

AND

RICHARD J. PASSANTINO A.I.A.

A REPORT SUPPORTED BY A GRANT FROM THE EDUCATIONAL FACILITIES LABORATORIES

CONTENTS

ACKNOWLEDGMENTS

Educational philosophy and the practice of teaching, be they a manifestation of tradition or the results of modern research, are the most important formative factors in the design of school buildings. It is, therefore, natural and necessary that every country will search for new means of improving its education and educational facilities according to its own beliefs and findings.

The value of international exchange of these new developments was impressively demonstrated to us during the course of this brief study of urban educational facilities in Europe. We were not only surprised by the abundance of useful information, but were also encouraged by the eagerness and hospitality of foreign architects and school administrators to establish such lines of communication.

Any publication owes much of its interest to the valuable contributions made by those individuals who, in addition to furnishing the necessary graphic material, have given so freely of their time and energy. We wish to acknowledge the response of our foreign colleagues, without whom these impressions could not have taken on substance in the form of this report. We wish to thank Mr. R. W. Ferguson and Mr. Perkins of the London County Council for their valuable recommendations on schools and for providing us with certain statistical information in London.

In Paris we received valuable information on European schools from Mr. John Beynon of the school building unit at UNESCO. Our tours of Zurich were arranged with much forethought by Mr. Herms, Secretary of the School Bureau. A most stimulating interview with Professor Alfred Roth of the Federal Technische Hochschule, Zurich, gave us valuable insight into European educational and architectural patterns.

Much information in Hamburg was gained at the Hochbauamt of the Baubehörde, through its Educational Director, Mr. Dressel, its Architectural Director, Mr. Gropp, and Mr. Sielaff of the educational staff who personally escorted us to all schools visited in Hamburg.

Our first stop in Stockholm was the Kungl. Skoloverstyrelsen, where Mr. Gustaf Hedenlund, architect SAR, and Mr. A. Folthiem of the Educational Department supplied us with ample informational material and made all arrangements for our tours. We are especially grateful to architect Ake Lindquist for giving so generously of his and his staff's time for many details of this report pertaining to Sweden.

In Copenhagen several members of the Undervisningsministeriet were extremely helpful, notably Mr. Ipsen, Mr. Kortzen, Mr. Noer, and Mr. Koch. Mr. Hansen, advising architect to the School Ministry, gave valuable assistance by his suggestions on our itinerary.

After our return to Washington, D. C., we were greatly aided in the translation of foreign manuscripts and drawings and furnished with most useful supplementary material by Mr. Carlo Christensen, Cultural Counselor of the Danish Embassy; Mr. Nils-Gustav Hildeman, Cultural Attaché of the Swedish Embassy, and Mr. Lucas Burckhardt, Counselor of Cultural Affairs at the Embassy of Switzerland.

To Mr. Pettengill and his staff at the A.I.A. Octagon Library goes our appreciation for the assistance in locating research material prior to our trip. We are indebted to Mrs. Erika Passantino for her translations of material for the Swiss and German sections, and to Mr. Thomas C. Witherspoon for editorial services.

We owe thanks to the staff of McLeod, Ferrara and Ensign, Architects A.I.A. for assistance with graphic material, proofreading, and overall encouragement, and to Miss Cathie McLeod for typing the seemingly never-ending amounts of manuscript.

JOHN W. McLEOD, F.A.I.A.
RICHARD J. PASSANTINO, A.I.A.

February 1968

THE STUDY...

ITS INTENT AND PURPOSE

There is probably no doubt in the minds of most Americans that U.S. school buildings are the best in the world. By and large this is true, if one takes into account only the newer crop of school buildings, particularly those that serve our burgeoning surburban areas. The overriding concern with this particular segment of the population stems naturally from the vast numbers of people involved and the shift of young married people away from the city to homes of their own in the suburbs. New homes require new schools and new school buildings, and an intelligent, educated, and prosperous young citizenry demands and is willing to pay for good education and good buildings for its children. This is a source of the pride we take in our new school buildings, the buildings which foreign school people visiting our country so highly praise and oftentimes copy, the buildings which are written about and publicized in journals and exhibitions throughout the world.

Our city schools and school buildings, have, by contrast, fared rather badly. Population shifts within the city have caused overcrowding in some schools while other areas have half-filled buildings. This, and other social and economic factors, make it difficult to justify new buildings, and the staggering cost of sites and ever-increasing costs of construction oftentimes cause deferral or abandonment of programs for sorely needed facilities.

Despite the discouragements encountered in large cities, school administrators, architects, and planners continue to explore scores of approaches to likely solutions for urban school-housing problems. Leased space in housing developments, especially designed joint-use facilities for combined school and commercial use, development of plans for building schools on "air-rights" space over roads and highways, and high-rise schools on small sites, are a few of the ideas suggested, and in some cases planned, as possible answers to the large cities school-housing dilemmas.

Recognizing that much of our culture and educational philosophy has its roots in the countries of Western Europe, and acknowledging that most of the older cities of Europe have been dealing with the problems of urban blight for many more years than we have, it appeared that a study of recent developments in school building in these countries might offer some valuable guidelines for the cities of the United States. Surprisingly, very little material has been published in U.S. journals, educational or architectural, with respect to new developments in the planning of urban schools in Europe. In Europe itself little effort seems being made to exchange views on this particular and vital aspect of schoolhouse planning, bound up as it is with the whole problem of life in large cities. In view of this country's close ethnic and cultural ties to Western Europe, it seemed to the authors entirely reasonable to suppose that a study of school buildings in the large urban centers of Europe would provide at least some interesting insights into design and planning concepts abroad, and might point the way to some significant breakthroughs in the handling of U.S. urban school building problems. The Educational Facilities Laboratories gave evidence of its interest in the total problem by providing a grant for the study tour. As travel time was restricted by the pressure of the authors' business interests at home and by other factors, the study was limited to five urban centers, London, Zurich, Hamburg, Copenhagen and Stockholm. These cities, it appeared from preliminary research, offered a good cross-section of Europe's school building effort and gave some promise of providing examples of school planning that might have significance for architects and school people in the United States.

It should be noted that the study was purposely limited to schools in the more densely populated sections of these cities. This self-imposed restriction was somewhat disconcerting to many of our school and architect contacts in Europe, who were eager to show us their newest schools, located, often as not, in outlying areas of the city or the suburbs. Hopefully, this will help dissuade those who might conclude that the case-study schools used are isolated examples of "showcase" school buildings. It is perhaps true that the buildings shown are better than average, but this, it seems to us, is a result of better than average educational and architectural thinking and talent rather than a deliberate attempt on our part to make something "special" out of these particular projects.

It should be noted, however, that the school buildings used herein as case study examples are the best that our study tour disclosed. By "best" we do not mean "best looking," but simply that these schools solved a particular problem in a first class manner, or, in some instances, developed a new approach to an old problem, or again, provided an educational environment which must surely have lifted the spirits of both students and teachers.

As a result of a short but intensive study of some 50 school buildings in the five cities visited, we believe the examples that follow are fairly representative of the caliber of work being done in the cities of Europe. Whether solutions developed in Europe will have any significant application to the problems of U.S. cities remains to be seen. U.S. school personnel and architects can, however, take heart from the vigor and dedication of their counterparts in the cities of Europe. Just as many of us in the U.S., they are striving to resolve problems that have been too long with us and have received too little attention.

THE URBAN PROBLEM. . . its cause and effect

In the United States the problems now being faced by large urban centers are of fairly recent origin. Only in the past few decades have we had to turn our attention away from the simple patterns of growth and expansion to the more pressing, and vastly more complex, problems of slum clearance, redevelopment, and revitalization of the central core of our large cities.

It was a simple matter in times past for the "better" citizens, their businesses, and their educational institutions to move "uptown," and outward, in order to maintain the status for which their increasing affluence provided the means. There was always a large reserve of respectable and up-coming groups of "lesser" citizens, many of them hardworking and ambitious immigrants, ready to take over the slightly used but still adequate buildings and facilities. Far from being frowned upon, this state of affairs was accepted as a normal pattern for the social and economic growth of a young nation on its way to greatness. Within the city proper this growth pattern served well enough, until the upward movement slowed and the impact of "status-quo" began to have its effect. This condition operated against those at the bottom of the social and economic scale and tended to restrict their opportunities for betterment, while at the same time confining them to areas of the city that by now had lost their respectability, and, in fact, were beginning to show signs of obsolescence and physical decay.

Unfortunately, but all too naturally, education and its physical facilities followed somewhat the same general patterns. The newer areas got the new schools and hence attracted the better teachers; the older schools got older and became increasingly less adaptible to new educational techniques, inevitably discouraging rather than challenging all concerned in their use.

With the great depression of the 1930's came a change in public attitude toward the problems of the disadvantaged, and the era of rugged individualism was replaced with a growing public awareness that the problems of each citizen were the responsibility of all citizens. Government initiative in the fields of public housing and community facilities was the first sign of a wholly new aspect of the social conscience of a maturing nation.

It would be encouraging to report that the problems so vigorously attacked in the 30's no longer exist today, but this is far from being true. A ten-year halt in new construction, caused by the depression

and lengthened by World War II, only aggravated the conditions in the cities and caused to be maintained in service dwellings and school buildings that should have been replaced long ago. The population explosion and flight to the suburbs which took place subsequent to World War II served to further increase the plight of the central city, enlarging the dimensions of the problem to the point where solutions that once might have alleviated some of the woes, were now so inadequate as to make them totally ineffective against the enormous breadth and depth of the whole problem and the people inextricably caught in its grasp. As the problem increases, those concerned with its solution are seeking answers not only possible and feasible at once, but which can serve to reverse the continuing deterioration of the cities' physical facilities and prevent the further disintegration of the moral fiber of its human resources. The solutions, then, need to be both bold and all-encompassing.

URBAN SCHOOLS IN EUROPE. . .

New Schools in the "old" country

Some General Observations:

It would be both presumptious and unfair to attempt to draw any broad comparisons between school buildings in Europe and those of the United States. Even limiting consideration to urban schools, such comparisons as could properly be made would serve no useful purpose and might in the final analysis divert attention from the real purpose of the study: to explore new approaches to the planning of school buildings in urban centers. The true measure of success, insofar as a particular design or plan arrangement is concerned, is how well the finished product serves the purpose for which it was designed, and, beyond this, what influence the building design has had on the neighborhood and the people living there. The physical appearance of a new school building can, by the very nature of its aesthetic appeal, bring about a renascence of self-respect in a rundown neighborhood. This yardstick can be applied to any urban school building, irrespective of country and without regard to its cost. Admittedly, cost is a significant factor in determining the ultimate appearance of any building, but aesthetic appeal and spiritual uplift are more a matter of creativeness than of money.

It became abundantly clear, very early in the study, that urban school building problems in the large cities of Europe are, in almost every respect, identical with those facing U.S. cities. The differences are really only a matter of degree rather than of kind. While in the United States the twin problems of population expansion and urban decay have created the major dimensions of the problem, some cities in Europe have had the added burden of dealing with the damage and destruction during World War II of hundreds of school buildings. In London alone 1150 school buildings were partially or wholly destroyed as a result of wartime bombing. Similarly, Hamburg suffered loss or damage to 60 percent or more of its school buildings. It is greatly to the credit of both these cities that, while their early postwar efforts were simply to build schools as rapidly as possible—which meant much temporary construction and repetitious use of standard elements—they are today developing designs that seek conscientiously to accommodate new contemporary educational programs, and at the same time producing schemes and designs of a high order of excellence, and in so doing, setting a pattern for neighborhood redevelopment.

While we believe broad comparisons between countries would be futile, it is still possible and quite desirable, to explore certain areas of similarity in order that those concerned with the urban school problem in the United States may profit by past and present experiences in Europe. This is not meant to suggest that approaches or solutions developed in Europe will necessarily have application here, but it oftentimes happens that the merest germ of an idea can stimulate a chain of thought that may well develop into a scheme, or solution, perhaps not even remotely resembling the original idea but nevertheless sparked by it.

SITES:

European cities are faced with the same problems of high land values and unavailability of large open spaces in the central areas of the cities. Speaking generally, it would seem that urban school sites are in most cases somewhat smaller than is the rule in U.S. cities. This is due, in large measure, to the fact that outdoor spaces for athletic activities are generally quite minimal and that parking space for automobiles is almost nonexistent, at least for student parking. These omissions, however, are not always the result of physical site limitations but are often based on the expressed policy that competitive sports are an extra-curricular community activity and not a school's responsibility. Similarly, student parking is not considered to be within the purview of educational administration and no site space is reserved for it.

The London schools have provided an innovation which will be noted here, although it is discussed in more detail later. As a supplement to whatever small play area may be provided at the individual school, a number of school or sports parks have been provided on the outskirts of the city where children from high density areas are bussed for one half day a week to participate in a full program of outdoor sports. Some four or five schools have joint, although separate, use of these facilities, which are maintained solely for school use.

In Europe, it is not uncommon to find more than one school occupying the same site. This practice, now being much discussed in the United States as the educational "park" or "plaza" idea, appears to be most highly developed in the Altona-Königstrasse school in Hamburg, where two complete schools, a youth (teen-age) center and a center for adult education and retired persons activities, are planned —and already partly constructed—as a single complex in the midst of a redevelopment area. Also we find an example of school-commercial use of the same site in Zurich, where the Canton Bank is occupying a wing (specifically designed for the purpose) of a new girls vocational school close to the downtown area. Again, we find in Stockholm

two completely independent girls vocational schools, placed one above the other, piggy-back style, in order to preserve sufficient ground area to provide an arcade of retail shops which sell the products of the schools and at the same time, permit the students to experience at first-hand the principles and practices of distributive education.

The few examples cited above and the many others illustrated below give some idea of the vigor and initiative being used to surmount the difficulties posed by the problems of limited sites for urban schools. A particularly ingenious solution, and a distinguished one, is the development at the Acland Burghley School in London of a "plaza" or "raft" by building over several sets of depressed railroad tracks. The present site, occupied by an obsolete, although still occupied, old school building, covers 1¼ acres. The construction of a new deck over the adjacent railroad tracks will add some 1⅓ acres to the site and with additional acquisitions permit the construction of a new school building to replace the old, providing a more adequate ground area totaling 5 acres.

PLANNING APPROACHES:

More than any other city visited, London gave evidence of interesting concepts in planning for education. It is apparent that British architects and educators are particularly concerned with the development of designs and schemes that are precisely tailored to fit new curriculum ideas and teaching techniques. The already familiar "house" system in British secondary school education, which is not unlike our "schools-within-a-school" concept, has been developed and refined to the point where it is almost the accepted form for secondary school design, even in "high-rise" structures.

The "house" concept in planning is fairly well exemplified in the three secondary schools illustrated. The Beaufoy school is a most interesting example, and the headmaster's own description of the educational "goals" to be achieved in this new facility, as given later in the text for this particular case study, gives some indication of the planning challenges which faced the architect for this project.

The "cluster" plan arrangement of small units in the Battersea elementary-primary school is an excellent example of planning with a purpose. Here the architect has used a grouping of small classroom elements arranged around open courts in such a way as to provide a delightful educational oasis in an overpowering urban desert of high-rise middle class apartment blocks. The tent-like roof pattern of the cluster acts as a visual foil for the monotony of the apartments and must surely, consciously or not, give a "lift" to children and perhaps even to their parents.

Another, and totally different, influence on planning and design is the still persistent preoccupation of most architects and school administrators in Europe with daylight as a primary source of classroom lighting. In almost all cases electric lighting is considered a supplement to natural lighting and hence is well below the foot-candles levels accepted as normal in the United States. The effect this daylight criterion has on plan arrangements is apparent, and it does create some problems in urban situations by dictating a greater ratio of building ground coverage to open space than would seem necessary. In this same vein, though, it should be noted that European architects tend to accept, and respect, site peculiarities and irregularities. Planning solutions are seldom dependent on the bulldozer as a site equalizer. Some fine examples of sensitive planning on difficult sites are to be found in Zurich; particularly noteworthy in this respect is the Kantonschule Freudenberg.

HIGH-RISE SCHOOLS:

European architects are not averse to high-rise solutions to urban school building problems. In fact, six to eight and ten story schools are fairly common in almost every city visited. Typically, the high-rise portion of the building houses the academic and related classrooms, while the specialized areas—library, cafeteria, gymnasiums, offices, etc.—occupy a one or two story base structure surrounding or set off from the tower.

The use of high-rise structures makes for some interesting planning solutions, as for example in the piggy-back arrangement at the Yrkes Skol in Stockholm. Here the independence of the two schools within the same structure is maintained by the simple expedient of providing two sets of elevator banks, each set assigned to serve its own school. In London both the Sarah Siddons school and the Tudor school use a skip-stop elevator arrangement that permits different space accommodations on alternate floors and can, thereby, provide a degree of flexibility in grouping large and small classes.

Another interesting high-rise solution is to be found in Zurich at the Hauswirtschaftliche Fortbildungsschule. Although the school is seven stories high, the main entrance, which is on the high side of the site and at the fourth floor level, is made a feature of the design: the designer has created an almost completely open arcade and achieved a stunning architectural and visual composition.

The use of a tower structure provides some side benefits, as for example in the Sarah Siddons School in London, which has several rooftop outdoor classrooms or observation areas that give a commanding view of London and its historical landmarks for the students' study and edification. In the Yrkesskola in Stockholm, the school's gymnasium is located on the roof, with the side roof areas designed as outdoor exercise areas.

PHYSICAL EDUCATION:

Facilities for physical education are, as noted previously, treated somewhat less ambitiously in Europe than in the United States. This is a result of a somewhat different point of view as to the relationship of body building and competitive sports in the educational curriculum. Physical education is never overlooked, however, it is simply treated as an integral part of the educational process, nothing more. In fact, it may well be that the square foot area of building space assigned to physical activities in the average European secondary school would equal or exceed that of a similar high school in the United States. What is missing is the large basketball arena with its seating arrangements for a thousand or so spectators. In place of this, however, are found as many as three or four exercise rooms completely equipped with all the paraphernalia of body building, climbing ropes, bars, ladders, rings, etc. Most of the newer secondary schools in London have in addition a fairly large paved space, enclosed all around, but with a series of folding or rolling doors for year-round use; the space is apparently used as a place for the students to "let off steam" or to curb an excess of youthful energies.

Swimming instruction appears to be part of the schools' regular curriculum; in many cities of Europe year-round facilities are part of a city wide program. In Hamburg a program is well under way to provide a new swimming pool unit at every fifth elementary school, located to serve a specific neighborhood area. It is expected that this program will require the construction of forty swimming pool buildings to complete the city wide coverage. It is interesting to note that the decision was made to incorporate swimming instruction into the educational curriculum at the elementary rather than at the secondary level.

VOCATIONAL EDUCATION:

Historically, Europe has given a great deal of attention to vocational training. Because of its traditional practice of separating academic and vocational students at an early age, 10 or 11 years, a highly developed vocational program has kept in step with the more academically oriented curriculum. Because of this, facilities for vocational education for both boys and girls are extensive and well organized.

Hamburg, in particular, has very complete facilities for teaching some forty trades, and, in some cases, a complete building is devoted to one or two specific and related trades. The Yrkesskola for girls, in Stockholm, specifically designed for needlecraft and homemaking,

has a group of shops, as mentioned earlier, where the schools' products are displayed and sold.

Discussions with a number of school officials in Europe disclosed that there are beginning to be doubts about the wisdom of such a single purpose vocational program as now exists, and particularly the early-age determination of a child's educational aims and goals. The feeling was expressed that a greater mix of academic and vocational subjects would provide a more realistic approach to today's and tomorrow's complex needs, both social and economic. Thus we find Europe, with its tradition of emphasis on vocational education, now reconsidering its objectives, while the United States, which has been inclined in the past to downgrade vocational subjects, is now deeply engrossed in the process of improving their educational status.

BOMB SHELTERS:

Many of the countries of Western Europe require the inclusion of underground bomb shelters in school facilities. These are generally planned as separate, single purpose shelters, built to protect the occupants from blast as well as fall-out. As far as we could observe, no other use is made of these shelter spaces, although, as in the Riedhof Schule in Zurich, the ground area above the shelter is sometimes designed as a playground.

CONSTRUCTION PRACTICES:

The materials and methods of construction in the school buildings of Europe are quite similar to those of the United States. Brick, concrete, steel, and wood are the usual building materials; by virtue of this any regionalism in architecture tends to disappear. This, unfortunately, is just as true of school building in the United States, particularly in the large urban centers. National building codes and fire safety regulations, by the broad sweep of their application, discourage many local, but nevertheless interesting, design possibilities and foster clean, simple, but oftentimes monotonous contemporary structures.

Most city schools in Europe are not nearly as restricted in planning for fire safety as in the United States. One can find handsomely designed open stairs as the focal point of a fine school entrance lobby, and open galleries as part of the traffic circulation pattern also provide excellent opportunities for creative planning and visual interest. The use of fine wood paneling in the public areas of a school certainly does much to enrich the visual environment of many European schools. European school officials we talked to, particularly those who had spent time visiting schools in the United States, agreed that our concern with building safety was too restrictive and over-emphasized. They pointed to their record of equally low incidence of fires in new schools as the basis for their beliefs.

We observed many construction technique developments in the field of component prefabrication. The already well-known British "CLASP" system of bulk purchase of standard mass-produced parts is still in use, although not in evidence in the large new London schools. Hamburg has for some years now made fairly extensive use of a system of precast concrete structural framing units incorporated into cruciform shaped four classroom unit buildings. This technique, and some recent newer developments, is discussed and illustrated in some detail in the Hamburg case study section of this report.

AESTHETICS:

As architects practicing day by day in the field of school building design, the authors will be excused if they close this discussion with a subject close to their hearts—aesthetics and beauty in school building design.

From general observations made during the study tour, it appears fairly obvious that Europeans are generally more conscious of, or at least more receptive to, the idea that beauty has a place in the planning of a school building than are their U.S. cousins. This conclusion is reached not so much from any feeling that European schools are so much better, or more beautiful than ours, which indeed they are not, but rather from the fact that there is a general public acceptance and appreciation of those creative touches, that when added to an otherwise merely good design, make it an outstandingly handsome one.

By and large, school building design in Europe, as in the United States, runs the gamut in any city from fairly poor through average to outstandingly good. The difference is to be found in attitude rather than performance. It is refreshing to find, for example, that an architect in Europe is expected, even required, to deliver a complete design package when given a commission for the development of a school plant. His job is not considered finished until the last tree has been planted and the gardens completed with fountains turned on or statuary in place. Afterwards, supplementary acquisitions—paintings, furnishings or whatever—must have the architect's approval before they can be installed in "his" project.

Designs for new schools, particularly large and important ones, are often published and exhibited extensively, and considerable public and press discussion of design character and aesthetic appropriateness frequently occurs, before a building takes shape. In fairness, this may be due to the fact that the public generally, has little to say about the location, cost, or method of financing school buildings—these are usually governmental decisions—and, in consequence, public responsibility is limited to discussion of the physical aspects of a proposed school. There is, nevertheless, evidence of keen public interest in the visual aspects of school building, and an apparent concomitant interest in having a school provide the finest cultural environment a community can afford. The opinions of numbers of school officials of this aspect of European school design can best be summed up in the words of one of them: "If art and beauty are part of our culture, where is there a better place for children to learn about them, and live with them, than in their own school."

14

Lion Kaye   Bellins gate

LONDON

3

Like other large urban centers in Europe, London faced a myriad of postwar reconstruction problems. Traffic congestion, extensive war damage, population increases, and uncoordinated vehicular expansion all contributed to a shortage of school facilities and the problems of future expansion. In addition, technological advances in teaching methods have rendered prewar schools obsolete to serve adequately modern educational as well as environmental needs.

Of the 1200 school buildings in use within London in 1939, war damage, ranging from very slight to total destruction was received by 1150. The London County Council, the education authority for London since 1904, was faced with a frantic need for postwar school places and attempted to solve the problem by regrouping what remained and hurriedly planning new facilities.

The County of London consists of 117 square miles, and land costs within the areas of the downtown schools are prohibitively high. An additional 1800 acres of land were purchased outside the County to provide athletic playing fields for city children. These sites are used by schools whose pupils spend a few hours per week traveling to and playing on the fields, traveling expenses being paid for by the Council. In addition, facilities are hired or leased on a number of play spaces in or near London.

This solution underlines a major problem in the city: 95 percent of the urban schools have no playing fields, although tennis courts are frequently provided. The very acute housing shortage inhibits adequate school land procurement (it costs The L.C.C. $2,240 per person to rehouse residents from an intended site) and gives rise to some ambitious engineering solutions for reclaiming urban land. Frequently housing and school planning must be encompassed within a unified larger development and many such Comprehensive Development Area (C.D.A.) programs are presently under study.

The obvious impression given by the site plans illustrated in this report would be total reliance on bicycle, city transit, or walking to serve the students' transportation needs since "car parks" are only provided for faculty use. An increasing number of secondary school students, however, do use motor cars, and frequently the on-street areas neighboring such schools are saturated with school parking. Free L.C.C. transportation within the city relies almost entirely on the public system and is dependent on the commuting distance as follows: 3 miles for seniors, 2 miles for juniors, and 1½ miles for infants. Every effort is made to place students in schools within this range. Handicapped children are always provided with the necessary transportation.

A major revision of London education was initiated by the Butler Act of 1944, which clearly established two stages of education: primary up to age 11 and secondary thereafter. All normal school fees were abolished and financing procedures for building and maintenance were streamlined to assist the total school system. At that time the functions of the Board of Education were transferred to a Minister who would also have registrational and inspectional jurisdiction over independent and private schools.

In London, the rules of "Management and Articles of Government" stipulate that the Council shall determine the general educational character of the school and its place in the Council's educational system. The headmaster or headmistress, in consultation with the managers and governors, has the duty of exercising the operation of the school's administration and curriculum. This includes internal organization, discipline, choice of books, methods of teaching, and the arrangement of classes. To help defray the costs of alteration and repairs these managers receive grants from the Ministry of Education.

A brief outline of the London school system may be helpful in the analysis of the succeeding graphic material:

Primary Education, the lowest of the three stages of public education, through which 90 percent of the London children pass, is divided into three divisions:

1. Nursery school for ages 2 to 5. This is voluntary and at the present time limited to a small percentage of total applicants.

2. Infants school for ages 5 to 7½.

3. Junior school for ages 7½ to 11½. Juniors and infants are sometimes combined into a single school under one head if the total number of children does not exceed 400. In primary schools boys and girls are generally educated together. Approximately one third of these schools are operated on a part-time basis.

Secondary Education provides schooling for ages 11½ to 17 or 18. Usually these schools range in population from 750 to 2000.

Vocational Schooling can begin as early as 15 years of age and usually lasts to age 18. These schools are extremely flexible in programming and operate as full time, part-time, sandwich course, or night school. Older employed students usually attend one day per week.

Frequently schools will pool their accommodations and resources to make up for deficiencies of staff and equipment. Under this system, older pupils of one school may possibly attend a nearby school for one day each week to study a subject not available in their own school.

In addition to the above, there are many special schools in the London area which offer unusual services for students who must take their education apart from the other children due to handicap or social necessity. Many boarding schools, including orphanages, are maintained as well as remedial schools for the blind, deaf, subnormal, epileptic, maladjusted, physically handicapped, and delicate children. Every effort is made to return these students to the normal classes whenever possible. Special home or hospital classes are given for those requiring such services.

Of additional interest are the two centers for rural studies started by the Council in 1957 in semi-rural campsites of Surrey. These centers are laid out with permanent buildings equipped for summer and winter use and there are full classroom and boarding facilities. Each center can accommodate 240 students with teachers who stay for approximately two weeks, during which time theoretical seminars are conducted in combination with outdoor study. Under this program parents pay for a portion of the cost, the remainder being borne by the Council.

"The School Journey Association of London" is an organization which encourages and arranges educational field trips throughout England and the Continent, providing grants toward the financing of such trips.

On the following pages are presented several of the many schools visited in the London area which we consider to be of unusual interest to school planners.

A graph outline of the London school system is provided on the following page.

18

AGE STUDENT	THE SCHOOL SYSTEM IN LONDON, ENGLAND			SCHOOL GRADE		
19 +	UNIVERSITY					
18 – 19	SECONDARY SCHOOL	SECONDARY SCHOOL	VOCATIONAL SCHOOL	13		SECONDARY EDUCATION
17 – 18	SECONDARY SCHOOL	SECONDARY SCHOOL	VOCATIONAL SCHOOL	12		SECONDARY EDUCATION
16 – 17	SECONDARY SCHOOL	SECONDARY SCHOOL ⟷	VOCATIONAL SCHOOL	11		SECONDARY EDUCATION
		(SCHOOL LEAVING CERTIFICATE)				
15 – 16	SECONDARY SCHOOL			10		
14 – 15	SECONDARY SCHOOL			9		
13 – 14	SECONDARY SCHOOL			8	RETARDED CHILDREN (non-graded)	COMPULSORY EDUCATION
12 – 13	SECONDARY SCHOOL			7		
11 – 12	JUNIORS SCHOOL	(JUNIOR LEAVING CERTIFICATE)		6		
10 – 11	JUNIORS SCHOOL			5		PRIMARY EDUCATION
9 – 10	JUNIORS SCHOOL			4		
8 – 9	JUNIORS SCHOOL			3		
7 – 8	INFANTS SCHOOL			2		
6 – 7	INFANTS SCHOOL			1		
2 – 6	NURSERY SCHOOL	(OPTIONAL)		K		

ACLAND BURGHLEY SCHOOL
London, England

For many years this school, located in an industrial section of London along a permanent railroad right of way, steadily deteriorated. Each time a steam powered locomotive passed nearby, the combination of noise and vibration would momentarily interrupt classroom instruction (windows had to be open for required ventilation) while the building itself acquired layer after layer of sediment.

This impossible situation continued up to, during, and even two decades after World War II, but now, what for generations had been its most disturbing antagonist, becomes an unquestionable asset—the railroad track.

In its quest for more urban school land in the high population area of London, the London County Council tried the obvious: acquisition of adjacent land. However, land acquisition comes high, not only in cost of the real estate itself plus demolition of existing structures, but the city's very acute housing shortage presented a relocation problem. In London, a relocation allowance of 2,240 dollars is allowed, per person—a healthy slice off any educational budget. Since the pressure of expanding this facility for a coeducational population of 1350 students became too serious to ignore even momentarily, the L.C.C. began to investigate the possibility of air rights over the track itself and feasibility studies began. Even considering the extensive foundation work, noise conduction control, and vibration problems, the solution proved to be a sound one. To quell criticisms already built up against such a "way-out" solution, it was recognized that any soundproofed concrete ramp spanning the track would have to be carefully designed. As a matter of prudence it was decided not to put any academic space on the raft itself but to utilize it for playground, parking, gymnasia forecourt, and games hall. The problem was further complicated by the necessity of maintaining the old school in continuous operation during the 3 years required for construction. The concrete raft solution has been completed (to everyone's satisfaction), and construction on the main building and the fieldhouse is already under roof.

The total site including the concrete raft is five acres and latest estimates place the total cost at 1,688,400 dollars. The architects were Howell, Killick, Partridge and Amis.

Another innovation being used in England and now undergoing serious evaluation in the United States is the combination-school theory—one facility encompassing Lower, Middle, and Upper school groupings with common usage buildings: library, administration, arts and crafts, recreation areas, and large group assembly, all in close proximity to classroom areas. This plan is based on an approach designating one wing with five levels to each grouping. A greenhouse is located on the roof of the science tract. Faculty parking is provided as well as ample bicycle storage racks.

A school of this type utilizes an off-site recreational center such as BARN ELMS (described later in this report) for large scale athletic activity.

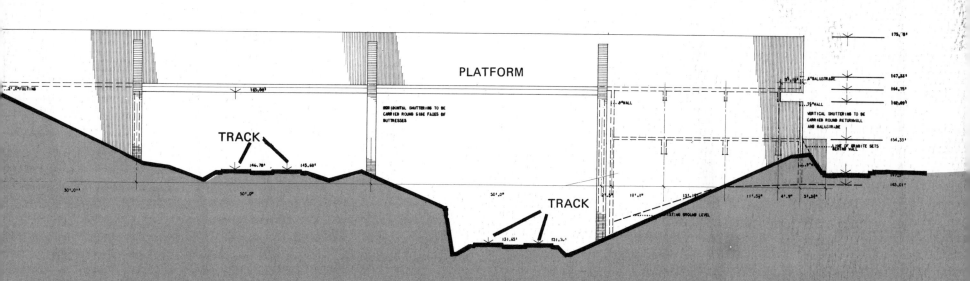

PLATFORM

TRACK

TRACK

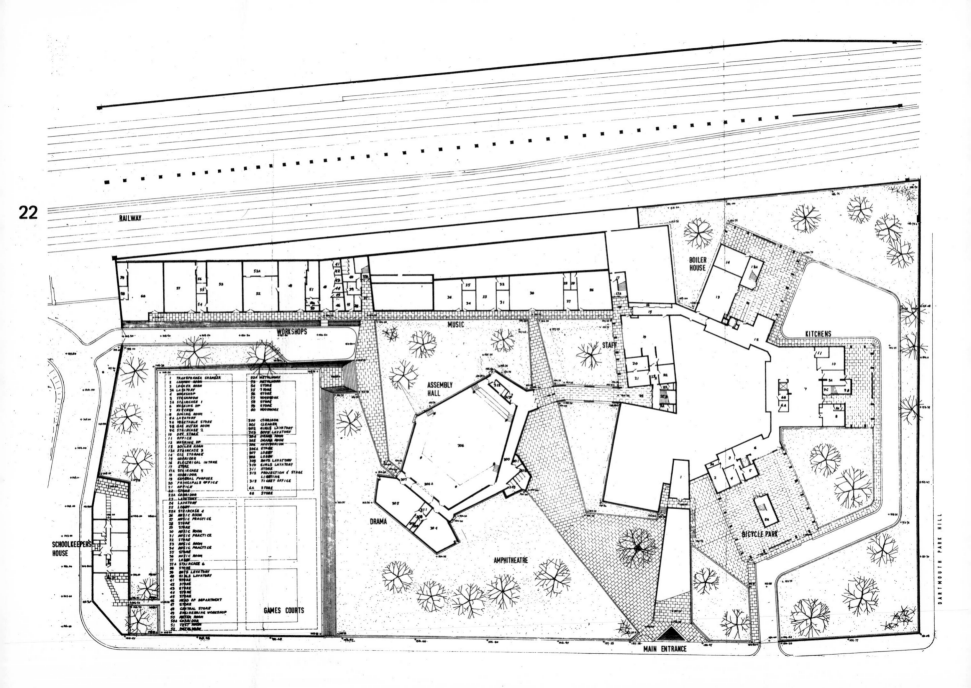

RAILWAY

BOILER
HOUSE

WORKSHOPS

MUSIC

KITCHENS

STAFF

ASSEMBLY
HALL

SCHOOLKEEPERS
HOUSE

DRAMA

BICYCLE PARK

AMPHITHEATRE

GAMES COURTS

MAIN ENTRANCE

DARTMOUTH PARK HILL

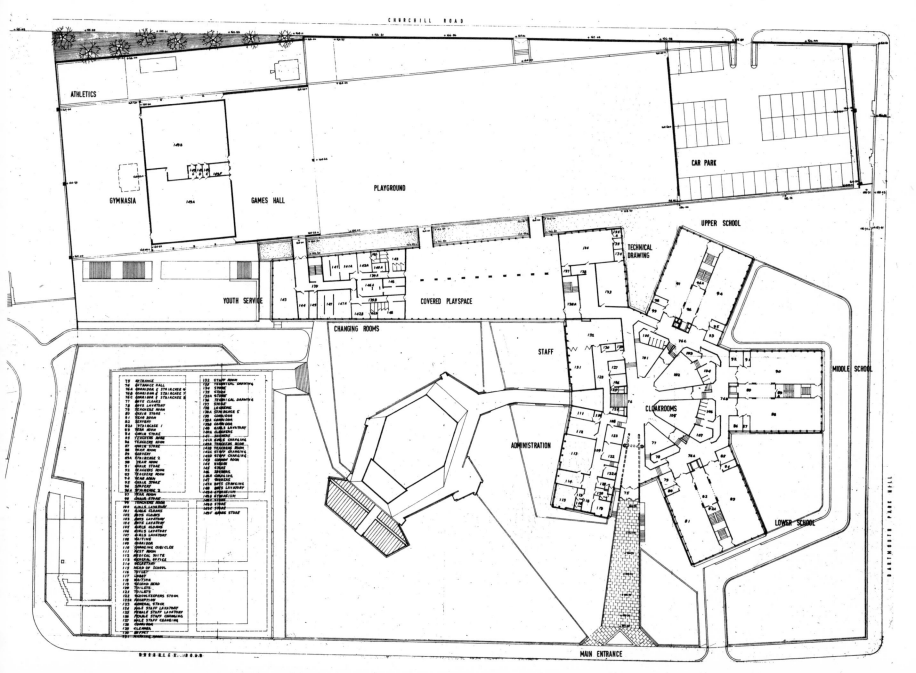

CHURCHILL ROAD

ATHLETICS

GYMNASIA

GAMES HALL

PLAYGROUND

CAR PARK

23

UPPER SCHOOL

TECHNICAL DRAWING

YOUTH SERVICE

COVERED PLAYSPACE

CHANGING ROOMS

STAFF

MIDDLE SCHOOL

CLOAKROOMS

ADMINISTRATION

LOWER SCHOOL

MAIN ENTRANCE

BEAUFOY
London, England

Completed in September of 1964, this facility on a six acre site accommodates 1400 male students (ultimately 1650) between the ages of eleven and eighteen in "house-group" units of 200. It was formed by combining two well-established schools.

The school is organized into eight houses of approximately 200 boys each, accommodated in a specially designed "house block" which provides facilities for dining, classroom instruction, club and group meetings. Throughout his eight-year stay each boy is placed under the charge of a tutor master as well as a house master, each of whom supervises his programs and development and notes his aptitude and abilities. (We observed that each student was known to these advisers on a first name basis.) At the end of the third year (form), the difficult choice of a course can be approached with a good deal of professional wisdom applied in advice to the boy and his parents. Additional guidance is obtained in collaboration with the careers master and youth employment officer. Should additional consultation be required the headmaster is available to the parents.

The "house blocks" are each oriented toward the course of study to which the student is allied, even though he may spend part of his day in other "blocks." Ideally "the facility should be one that boards the student as well," the headmaster feels, "and ultimately we shall have dormitories." There are art studios, music, commerce, metal and wood crafts, as well as science, mathematics, history, and geography areas with their specialized equipment.

There is a well stocked library, three gymnasia, a covered games area capable of being combined with an outdoor courtyard, tennis courts, cricket, soccer, and basketball courts, and a grassed athletic area. The large assembly hall is equipped for audio-visual presentations as well as orchestral and dramatic work.

"Specialization" does not begin until age 14. For the first three years all boys follow a "general" course including art, music, crafts, general science, and foreign language. These courses lead to the General Certificate of Education, Ordinary and Advanced levels in each field, as well as to The Certificate of Secondary Education at the age of sixteen. Boys are prepared for colleges of technology, universities, teacher training, craft apprenticeship, or commerce institutions. A great deal of emphasis is placed on physical training, and the boys are expected to participate in the wide variety of athletic programs under trained instructors, including fencing, judo, squash, ice skating, boxing, rugby, and long-distance swimming.

It was pointed out to us that European schools place as much if not more emphasis on individual participant sport as they do on the large group activity with its attendant dangers of oversophistication and commercialism. This does not, however, rule out representational "teams" that regularly compete with other schools, in the area and competitive spirit runs high. Physical education in the gymnasia, however, is a regular part of every boy's schedule. A comprehensive range of clubs and societies, musical and dramatic activities, school journeys, and educational visits are also organized.

This project was part of a larger C.P.A. plan and was built at a total cost of $1,820,000, with off-site recreation provisions. The architects were "The Architects Co-Partnership."

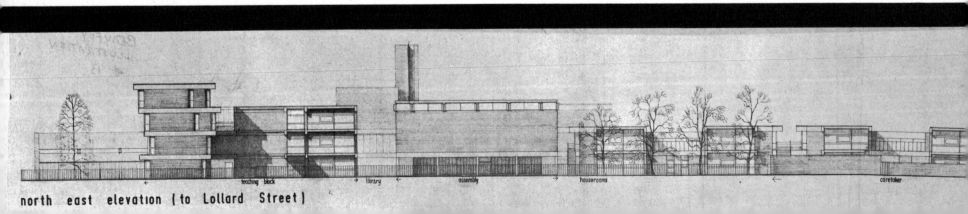

north east elevation (to Lollard Street)

teaching block   library   assembly   houserooms   caretaker

long jump

pole vault

house block   house room

classroom

chairs

kitchen

store   staff

equip store

chairs

classroom

clocks

house room

master

work stock common room
shop

bed

bed

bed

living

kitchen

caretaker

soccer

tennis

north

house room

clocks

master

classroom

chairs

store   staff

kitchen

equip store

chairs

clocks   classroom

house room

master

house block

car park

cricket nets

basketball

general science

advanced chemistry

preps.

chemistry

art room

preparation

art

evening institute

office

stock

principal

servery

music

foyer

general science

head   store   store   stock   sculpture

intake

music   music   music

science

weaving etc.

kiln

store

workshop

assembly hall

classroom

surgery   stock

consulting   waiting

classroom

entrance

classroom

clocks

gymnasium

store   store

gym.

head

gym.

fives courts

classroom

classroom

games hall

classroom   classroom

changing room

classroom

classroom   classroom

classroom   history

teaching block

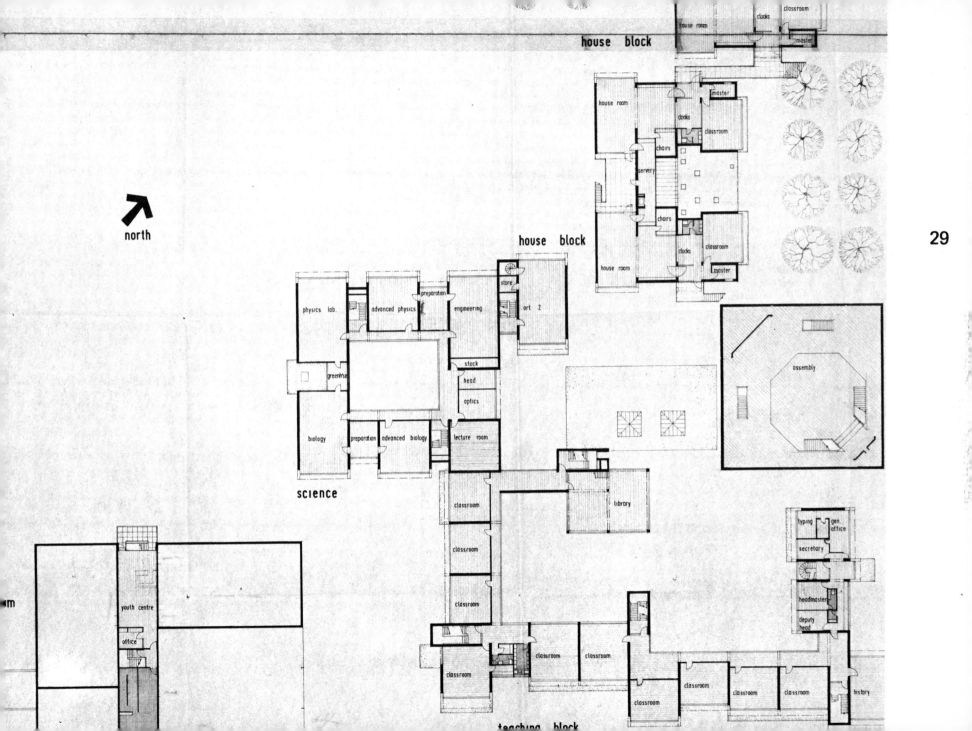

north

house block

house room

clocks

classroom

master

house room

master

clocks

classroom

chairs

servery

chairs

clocks

classroom

house room

master

house block

preparation

store

physics lab.

advanced physics

engineering

art 2

greenh'se

stock

head

optics

biology

preparation

advanced biology

lecture room

science

assembly

classroom

library

typing

gen. office

secretary

classroom

headmaster

classroom

deputy head

youth centre

office

classroom

classroom

classroom

classroom

classroom

classroom

classroom

history

teaching block

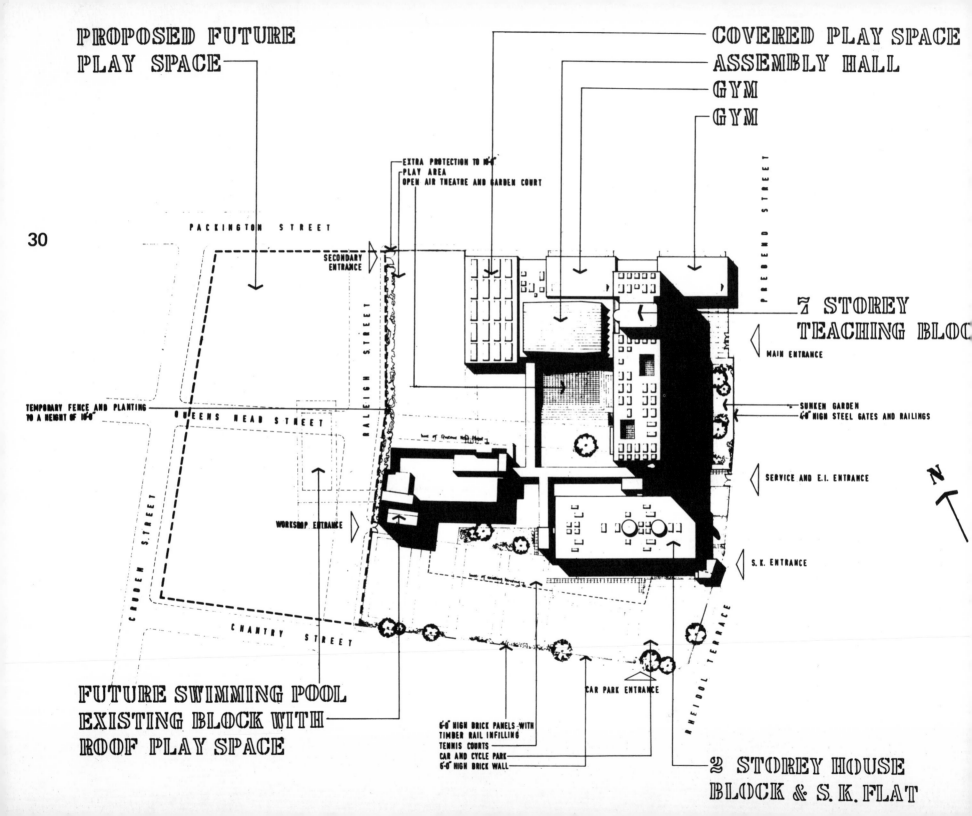

PROPOSED FUTURE
PLAY SPACE

COVERED PLAY SPACE

ASSEMBLY HALL

GYM

GYM

PACKINGTON STREET

EXTRA PROTECTION TO 16'-0"
PLAY AREA
OPEN AIR THEATRE AND GARDEN COURT

SECONDARY
ENTRANCE

7 STOREY
TEACHING BLOC

MAIN ENTRANCE

TEMPORARY FENCE AND PLANTING
TO A HEIGHT OF 16'-0"

QUEENS HEAD STREET

RALEIGH STREET

PREBEND STREET

SUNKEN GARDEN
4'-0" HIGH STEEL GATES AND RAILINGS

SERVICE AND E.I. ENTRANCE

N

WORKSHOP ENTRANCE

CRUDEN STREET

S. K. ENTRANCE

CHANTRY STREET

RHEIDOL TERRACE

CAR PARK ENTRANCE

FUTURE SWIMMING POOL
EXISTING BLOCK WITH
ROOF PLAY SPACE

6'-0" HIGH BRICK PANELS WITH
TIMBER RAIL INFILLING
TENNIS COURTS
CAR AND CYCLE PARK
6'-0" HIGH BRICK WALL

2 STOREY HOUSE
BLOCK & S.K. FLAT

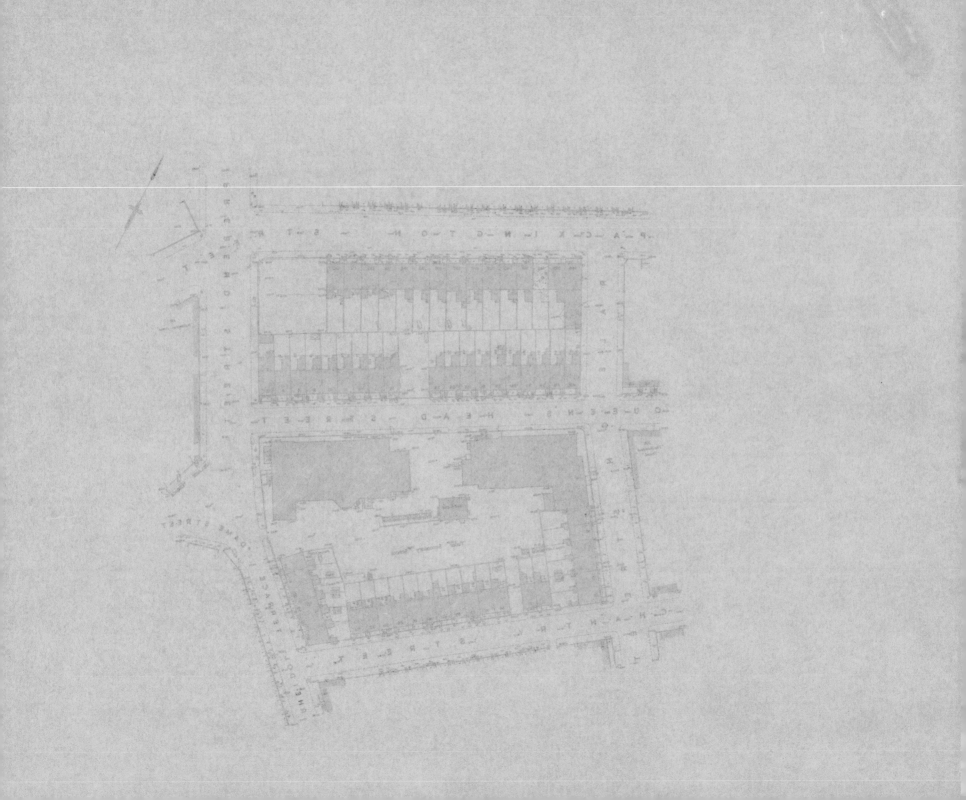

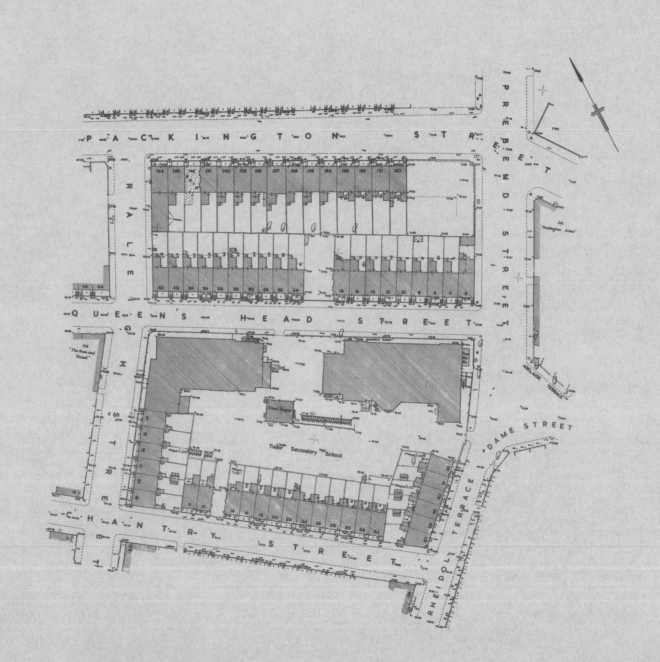

TUDOR SCHOOL
(Islington Green)
London, England

An often proposed but seldom achieved solution to the problem of obtaining sufficient urban real estate for an adequate school facility is the reclaiming of a dedicated right of way. This is never an easy remedy owing to the congested street patterns which must receive the added burden of the resultant traffic. A further obstacle is the inability of city traffic engineers and school planners to work homogeneously toward similar goals. However many such difficulties presented to the L.C.C. and the architects of the new Tudor School they were handily overcome. They were able to combine the existing school with a residential block on the other side of Queens Head Street which, added to the street area itself, created a super block of nearly four acres. Additional land has been acquired on the other side of Raleigh Street and the rare feat may be successfully invoked once more, as that street is incorporated for future play space and swimming pool, thereby adding an additional two acres of ground (see diagrams).

The old structure had to remain in continual use during construction and after being remodeled into technical shops was incorporated into the master plan.

The coeducational facility for 1290 secondary students between the ages of 11 and 17 boasts a well designed central forum—a sunken theatre garden which has direct access to the large architecturally featured assembly hall. The expanded site provided for several tennis courts, and parking for 15 faculty autos and 25 bicycles (most students walk or take free city transit to school). The standard covered games hall and two gymnasia are included, all elements being joined by covered walks.

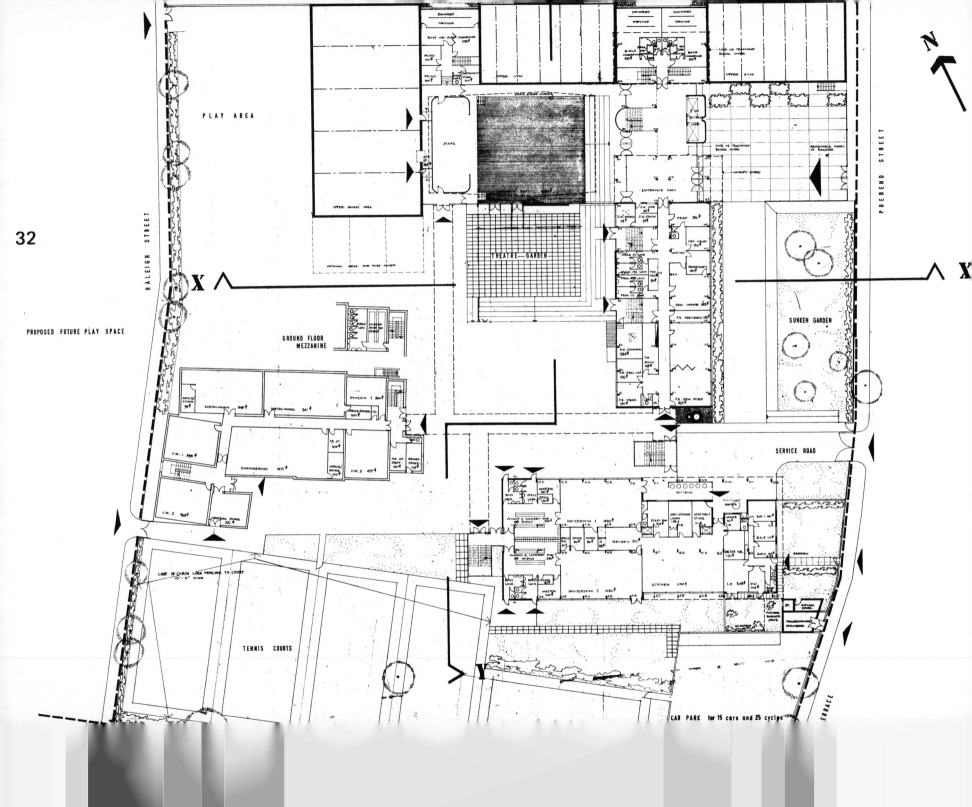

32

PLAY AREA

PROPOSED FUTURE PLAY SPACE

RALEIGH STREET

PREBEND STREET

X

X

THEATRE—GARDEN

SUNKEN GARDEN

GROUND FLOOR
MEZZANINE

SERVICE ROAD

LINE OF CHAIN LINK FENCING TO COURT
10'-0" HIGH

TENNIS COURTS

CAR PARK for 15 cars and 25 cycles

TERRACE

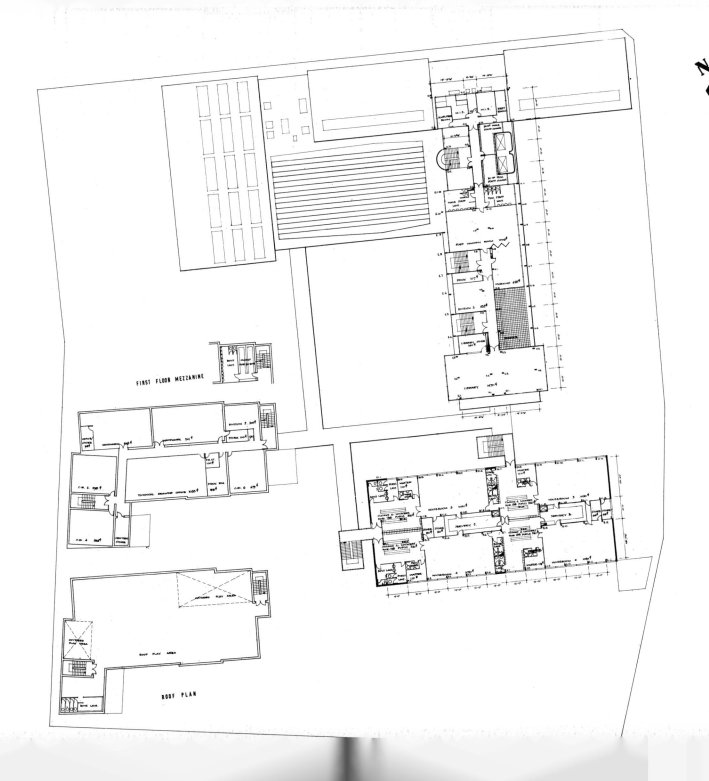

FIRST FLOOR MEZZANINE

ROOF PLAN

33

4TH FL.

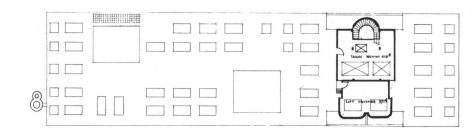

ROOF

34

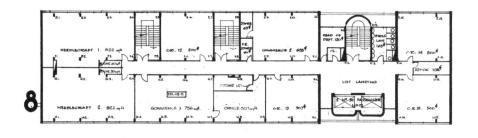

3RD FL.

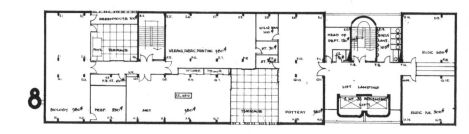

6TH FL.

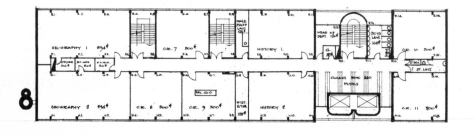

2ND FL.

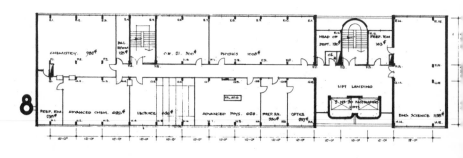

5TH FL.

A skip-floor elevator system is employed in the six level block, which utilizes the non-traffic areas of the alternate floor corridors as cloak rooms for students. The sixth floor biology area has an integral greenhouse open to the roof as well as an enclosed terrace with a magnificent screened view of London proper. A similar terrace occurs on the opposite side of the building in the arts and crafts suite. Domestic arts are housed in the two-story detached building to the south of the main block and a central library of 1470 square feet with outdoor terrace is located on the first floor above ground in the main block. The roof area of the existing remodeled building has been effectively transformed into usable play space.

The architects, Sherrer and Hicks, emphasized the plasticity of the concrete structure with strong use of sculptural form in the elevator walls, auditorium roof, skylights, and boiler stacks, which run free standing up the entire height of the high rise. This tight control of mechanical elements pays off handsomely in the resulting enhancement of the architecture rather than its destruction—an opportunity frequently overlooked by many designers. Art, where used, is effective, such as the large mosaic mural along the north exterior wall of the gymnasia.

This complex, exclusive of land purchase, cost 1,450,000 dollars including site improvements, or roughly $12.60 per square foot for main buildings. The construction period lasted slightly under two and one half years with occupancy in early 1965.

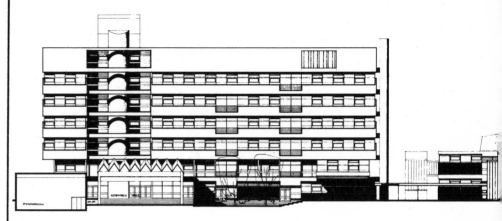

SECTION Y-Y

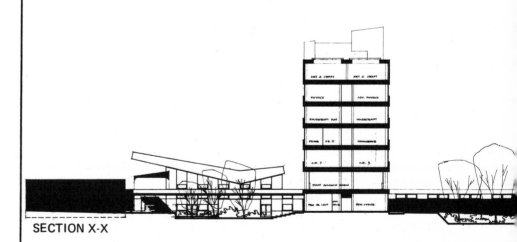

SECTION X-X

SARAH SIDDONS
London, England

The site of 4¾ acres is situated in a slum clearance area opposite Paddington Town Hall and Paddington Green, separated from them by Harrow Road, which is to be widened when the existing buildings between the road and the school will be demolished. The clearance of the site had to be in stages because of the rehousing problem and because only 1¾ acres to the east of the site were immediately available. There was an urgent need for new school places in this area.

Courses lead to the General Certificate of Education examination at ordinary and advanced levels; general and commercial, retail distribution courses, etc. are also provided. The school is organized in the house system with tutor groups.

The school was planned on the eastern part of the site and because of the need to economize in site coverage an eight story teaching block was designed. To the east of this block, which is on a north-south axis, is a two-story building, containing a main entrance for the girls on the ground floor, together with cloakrooms, etc., and the kitchen and service area. House rooms are planned round the assembly hall on the first floor and access from these to the teaching block is by means of enclosed bridges at this level. The three gymnasia are built on the western side of the tall block, close to the play spaces.

The construction is in situ reinforced concrete frame in the teaching block. The assembly hall is spanned by light steel trusses with a timber roof; the gymnasia building is in steel frame construction.

The main floor levels of the building are strongly emphasized by the thick horizontal bands of exposed aggregate slabs; the infilling panels are of softwood, painted white, metal windows are white, and the under window panels in grey glass. The end walls are faced in dark brick. The elevators do not serve the top or intermediate floors, so the engine rooms are almost buried in the top floor and do not form an important part of the silhouette.

Domestic sciences as well as liberal arts subjects are taught in this 1250 girl secondary school which houses one of the three existing city retail shops set up for sales training classes. Roof areas overlooking the city provide space for outdoor classes and minor exercising. This building was completed in late 1961 at a total cost of one million dollars for slightly under 100,000 square feet.

KEY:
2 Cycle Storage
3 Gymnasium
4 Teaching Block
5 Oil Storage
6 Assembly Unit
7 Play Space
8 Car Parking
9 Road Widening

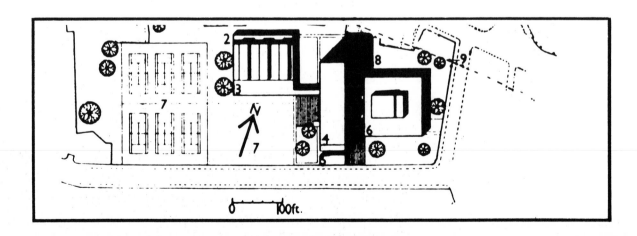

BATTERSEA PARK ROAD,
PRIMARY SCHOOL
London, England

The 1¾ acre site of this primary school for 560 juniors (mixed) and infants lies to the south of Battersea Park Road in an area now being extensively redeveloped with new housing by the Borough Council.

The school is organized in two departments: the infants' school has accommodation for 240 children and the junior school for 320 children. The plan is unusual for London in being entirely single story, a method which achieves flexibility, enclosed and semi-enclosed private paved outdoor teaching areas to nearly every classroom, and enables the school to look inwards and create its own environment.

Generally both the infants' and junior classrooms are planned in groups of three around a small lobby and sanitary accommodation. The groups of classrooms are linked by covered ways to the core of the school which consists of the two assembly halls planned side by side. Great economies were made in the circulation area and in the construction which enabled both infants and juniors to have a sep-

arate dining area as an annex to the hall. This area may be shut off by sliding doors, and by using movable platform units it may become a stage. Each department has its own administrative rooms and a library planned in one block accessible from the core. The kitchen is common to the dining areas. The gardens and courts are paved and planted.

The roofs of the classrooms are constructed of three layers of timber boarding covered with roofing felt and exposed internally. They are supported at only four points, which means that windows can be introduced into any external wall of the room. This, coupled with the pavilion type of plan, gives each room good lighting, an interesting and varied outlook, and an informal atmosphere. The interior walls are of white painted brick, with timber windows, cherry wood parquet floors, and natural wood ceilings. The assembly halls follow the same form of construction. Wherever possible the natural finish of the materials used was left internally as well as externally.

This contract was completed in 1963 at a total cost of $310,000, containing a total area of 24,600 square feet. The architect was Hubert Bennett, F.R.I.B.A.

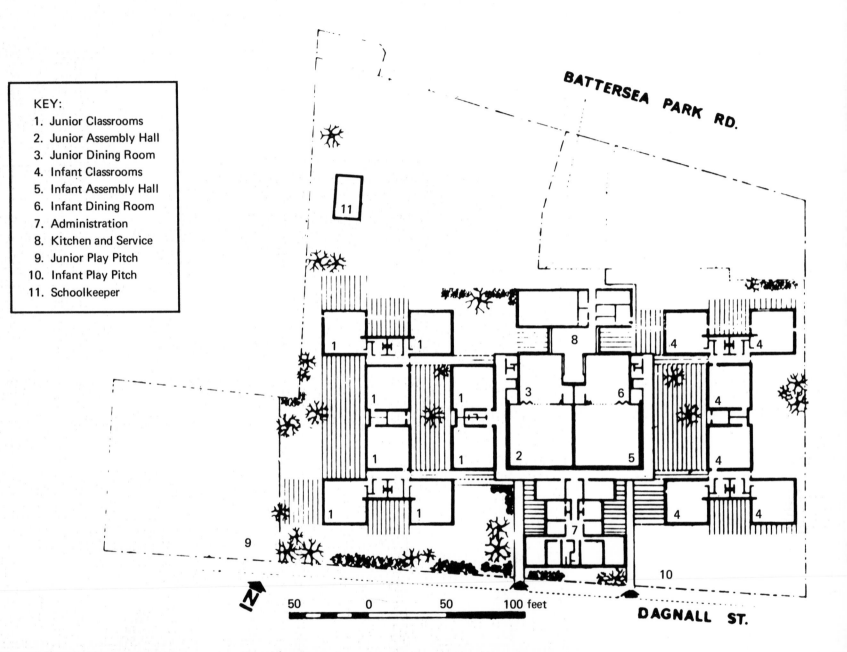

KEY:
1. Junior Classrooms
2. Junior Assembly Hall
3. Junior Dining Room
4. Infant Classrooms
5. Infant Assembly Hall
6. Infant Dining Room
7. Administration
8. Kitchen and Service
9. Junior Play Pitch
10. Infant Play Pitch
11. Schoolkeeper

BATTERSEA PARK RD.

DAGNALL ST.

50   0   50   100 feet

BARN ELMS SPORTS CENTER
Surrey, England

School parks are a common London solution for providing large grassed play areas and athletic facilities for urban schools that cannot utilize on-site space due to high land costs. Interdistrict contests in football, hockey, tennis, cricket, etc., are handled by local school sports associations staffed with serving and retired instructors. Several schools are assigned to each recreational area and students are bussed out for one half day per week of sports activities. Locker facilities are provided at the grounds.

The London County Council also owns a boat house on this Thames River site where boats and instruction are available to schools and youth organizations. All children, ten years of age or over, are encouraged to receive swimming instruction and usually the Council provides transportation to the nearest local pool. Some of the newer secondary schools were built with swimming pools. This facility completed in 1957 is utilized by 1000 children daily, providing locker accommodations for 300 boys and 210 girls.

Color, where used, is lively and all materials are designed for heavy duty usage. A first aid room is incorporated into the plan.

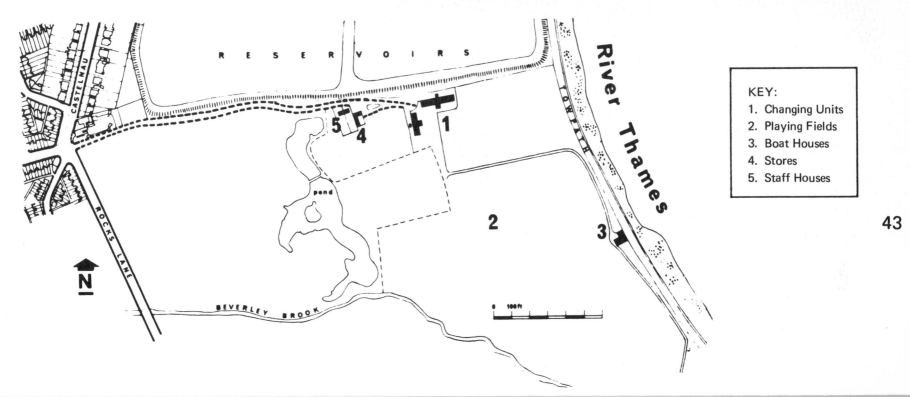

KEY:
1. Changing Units
2. Playing Fields
3. Boat Houses
4. Stores
5. Staff Houses

TIGURUM. Zürych.

ZURICH

LIMAT FLU

ZYRICH

Am Spitz.

A. Groß Münster.
B. Framen Munster.
C. St. Peter.
D. Prediger Closter.
E. Barfußer Closter.
F. Augustiner Closter.
G. Oetenbacher Closter.
H. Bibliothec.
I. Der Hofe.
K. Das Raht hauß.
L. Der Spital.
M. Das Kauff hauß.
N. Das Korn hauß.
O. Die Metzig.
P. Schützen hauß.
Q. Pappyrmühlen.
R. Rennweger thor.
S. Cappeler hofe.
T. S. Anna.
V. Uffdorffer thor.
X. Niderdörffer thor.
Y. Linden thor.
Z. Nemmarckt th.
✝. Ketzer thurn.
✱. Wolffs thurn.
↑. Geiß thurn.

4

"School buildings are the palaces of Switzerland." This often repeated quotation expresses the Swiss people's desire to have their schools provide the facilities and environment required to maintain the country's high educational standards. By nature the Swiss are democratically oriented, and this atmosphere filters down to even the smallest detail of school organization, a surprising accomplishment in view of the diversity in national origins of the people. The population of 5½ million includes about ½ million foreigners. Three major languages are not only in common use but must be used in all legal documents as well as in the laws of the land. In addition, most Swiss know at least one other foreign language, usually English. This small country with its dramatic landscape consists of only 10 million acres, approximately one-tenth the size of California, and is subdivided into 22 separate, and for the most part, autonomous districts called cantons. It is on this level of government that the Swiss have elected to place their authority, and many referendum mechanisms insure popular vote control of most major and minor issues. The canton, therefore, is solely responsible for the administration of its school system. The creation of a federal department for schools has twice been rejected by the people; national universities do exist, however, as well as Federal Institutes of Technology, such as the one in Zurich, for use by all the cantons. Since legal requirements as well as administrative policies do vary by area, this section of our study relates more specifically to Zurich, a city of 500,000 inhabitants and the major city of the canton.

Zurich has nine years of obligatory schooling, which carries the student through six years of lower school and three years of upper school, or approximately to the fifteenth year of age.

All schooling in Zurich is similar until the child is ten years old. At this point a major division occurs between vocational and academic training. (The sharpness and timing of this two-track system is the subject of much discussion in Switzerland, as it is elsewhere, and will not be elaborated upon here.) The academic students enter into "Gymnasium" at this point leading them toward a final degree (Matura), at about 21 years of age; afterward they eventually complete their studies at a major university, such as St. Gallen.

An alternative to the full academic curriculum occurs after approximately nine years of schooling and coincides with the end of compulsory education. This provides an intermediate diploma at age nineteen, prior to obtaining the Matura, and the student does not continue to a university.

Approximately 35 to 40 percent of Zurich's school population complete the vocational school program, 6 percent enter universities, and the balance completes a nonprofessional general curriculum education. (Many cantons have mandatory requirements concerning attendance at Continuation Schools.)

The students who follow the vocational pattern stay with elementary or secondary training during the compulsory period and then branch into the many diversified technical-vocational fields that lead to apprenticeship programs. Technical colleges exist for additional training after apprenticeship, and many future instructors at vocational schools take these extension courses.

The technical-scientific Middle schools provide for the preparation of professional engineers, architects, and scientists. Continuation schools beyond mandatory requirements are the rule in Switzerland, where only 5 percent of the students leave for manual work at this point.

Both boarding and nonboarding private schools are very prevalent in Switzerland. There are approximately 400 throughout the country and they are also under the academic control of the cantons. Many schools for handicapped children exist in each canton, for Swiss law provides for the training of every "educable" child even with a minimum I.Q.

Sizes of classes are kept to workable numbers in Zurich, ranging from 36 pupils in lower primary schools to 20 pupils in senior schools. The average secondary class has 26 pupils. Classes for slow or mentally retarded students are kept below these numbers, usually about 18 pupils, and these special schools comprise 5 percent of the student population.

Financing of school facilities is very much dependent upon the needs of the recipient. If there are a large number of students requiring a school plant in a city with a relatively poor tax base, the canton may provide up to three quarters of the financing for land purchase, construction, and upkeep. Zurich does not receive this much and consequently school expenditures account for over 25 percent of the municipal budget.

Nearly all construction of school buildings is awarded on an open competition basis with a professional jury of architects and school administrators presiding over the submittals. By Swiss law such buildings must be awarded to any competent practitioner who wins the competition (usually limited to local architects). Larger public buildings are national competitions with the most important of these going to international competition. After the jury selects a winner, the entries are publicly displayed and are the subject of much editorial concern. They then are "ratified" by public vote, which usually follows the jury's selection and suggested modifications. Swiss officialdom, as well as the general population, has very progressive ideas concerning new schools, and the system produces satisfactory results.

One aspect of school planning that helps to develop public involvement in design is the usage of the premises both by students and adults, in evening classes and cultural activities. Frequently, separate accesses and related services—snack bar, ticket booths, cloakroom services—will be designated to permit public use of auditoria for lectures, theatre, or musical events. Often the auditorium is a separate structure and does not interfere with the regular activities of the school itself. If connected with the school, it may also serve both as auditorium and cafeteria.

While staying in Zurich, we journeyed to neighboring Zug for a close look at one of the factories specializing in "prefabricated schools." This particular company has several plants in operation throughout Europe and has plans to franchise several others. The need for prefabrication in Switzerland is clear when the following factors are considered:

1. Construction Time: Small conventional schools frequently take up to two years to construct due to manpower shortage, difficult terrain, frequently impassable in winter, and negotiated changes in the work. Most construction stops completely for three months every year when many alpine roads are unpassable, and lack of materials supplies suspends operations.

2. Cost Certainty: Since Switzerland uses a form of the TENDER system (Quantity Survey) and the architect usually is the contractor for the work, a building does not have a "firm" contract price prior to construction nor are plans developed to "bidding document" clarity. Frequently the ultimate cost of a building will be 40 percent over the original estimate with the mortgage company a sympathetic onlooker.

3. Workmanship: Since Switzerland, like Germany, finds it difficult to meet manpower needs, foreign laborers are sometimes imported for this purpose. (Recently Switzerland has curtailed issuance

of working permits for migrant laborers.) Owners and architects have been rather discouraged by the inability of unskilled labor to maintain the high standard of construction required in Switzerland.

4. Overall Cost: The particular model shown us cost $12.00 a square foot, or approximately one third of conventional Swiss construction.

Labor Unions are nonexistent in Switzerland, and professional societies do not seem to oppose prefabrication as they do in other countries, since architects cross into the contractors' field. In spite of the influence of the above factors on their judgment, it is the considered opinion of most educators and architects in Switzerland that the completely "prefabricated school plant" is an evil to be avoided at any cost. Many associate it with emergency building programs necessitated all over Europe in the post World War II period. Perhaps the calmest judgment came from Professor Alfred Roth, Professor of Architecture at Zurich Technische Hochschule and the author of THE NEW SCHOOLHOUSE, now in its fourth edition. Professor Roth feels that prefabrication in his country is good only if it develops into a "component" system of small elements, although these elements could be as large as the classroom unit itself, but never the entire school. Many local laws and problems prevent a standardized solution, and planning as well as site development must always be left to the imagination of the architect. When we remarked about the cost differential, he again invoked the proverb that begins this chapter — "School buildings are the palaces of Switzerland."

AGE OF STUDENT	THE SCHOOL SYSTEM IN SWITZERLAND						SCHOOL GRADE	
	APPRENTICESHIP VOCATIONAL SCHOOL PREPARATORY TEACHER'S TRAINING SCHOOL PRACTICAL TRAINING SCHOOL		COMPLETION CERTIFICATE NOT ENTITLING TO UNIVERSITY STUDIES.			UNIVERSITY (HIGH SCHOOL)		
18 – 19			MIDDLE SCHOOL	MATURITY		MIDDLE SCHOOL	12	
17 – 18			MIDDLE SCHOOL			MIDDLE SCHOOL	11	
16 – 17			MIDDLE SCHOOL			MIDDLE SCHOOL	10	
15 – 16	ELEMENTARY SCHOOL	SECONDARY SCHOOL	MIDDLE SCHOOL				9	COMPULSORY EDUCATION
14 – 15	ELEMENTARY SCHOOL	SECONDARY SCHOOL	MIDDLE SCHOOL				8	
13 – 14	ELEMENTARY SCHOOL	SECONDARY SCHOOL	MIDDLE SCHOOL				7	
12 – 13	ELEMENTARY SCHOOL		MIDDLE SCHOOL		RETARDED CHILDREN (non-graded)		6	
11 – 12	ELEMENTARY SCHOOL		MIDDLE SCHOOL				5	
10 – 11	ELEMENTARY SCHOOL		MIDDLE SCHOOL				4	
9 – 10	ELEMENTARY SCHOOL						3	
8 – 9	ELEMENTARY SCHOOL						2	
7 – 8	ELEMENTARY SCHOOL						1	
6 – 7	ELEMENTARY SCHOOL						K	
5 – 6	KINDERGARTEN (OPTIONAL)							

HAUSWIRTSCHAFTLICHE FORTBILDUNGSSCHULE
Zurich, Switzerland

Community participation in matters of public interest is a deeply ingrained element of the Swiss way of life. Designers can be completely confident that the citizens will indeed congregate in public spaces for the exchange of ideas, the casting of votes, and the enjoyment of social or cultural events.

Such opportunities are richly provided in an area beautifully and conveniently located on a riverside site near downtown Zurich. In addition to a seven-level home economics school, this site is shared by a large city bank and administrative offices for the county government. These three facilities, though harmoniously integrated, have no interrelation of use, and, perhaps, have only one element in common: a desirable downtown location. An open plaza amid these three units serves as a unifying link while not impairing their autonomous function.

For the projected future the planners envision a "neighborhood commons" with small shops, kiosks, and a combination gymnasium-auditorium which can be used in conjunction with an outdoor stage. A small choral studio seating 140 vocalists is also programmed and, last but not least, a generously sized playground for neighborhood children who would be supervised by the young ladies of the school.

All in all, this project represents an impressive community package when visualized in its matrix of landscaped gardens, river promenades, and well used natural levels, which allow overlooks above covered walkways.

The school itself is an object lesson in European emphasis on careful training in the domestic arts. In the full-time program of day classes the school houses 400 to 500 young women between the ages of 16 and 20; the program of study, however, is also extremely popular with adult women, hence the school offers an extensive night school program as well.

A review of the floor plans will indicate the concentrated nature of the high-rise school. The kitchens are furnished with the latest electric and gas equipment, and the classrooms are used only for the theoretical instruction of home economics. Besides well-equipped sewing and ironing rooms, the school also provides classes for the instruction of child care. One vestige of European house care, all but extinct in America, is still taught within its specially designed spaces: the art of rug beating and its companion science, the daily airing of mattresses and comforters—an intriguing example of tradition respected by the modern architect.

49

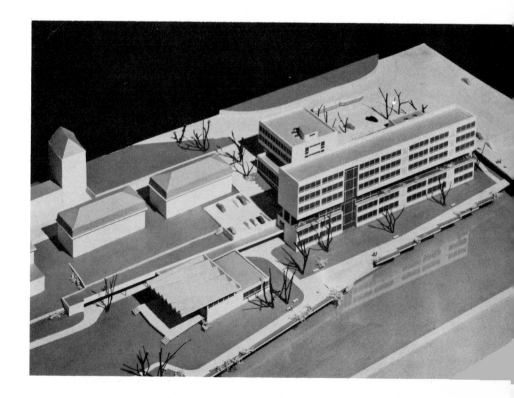

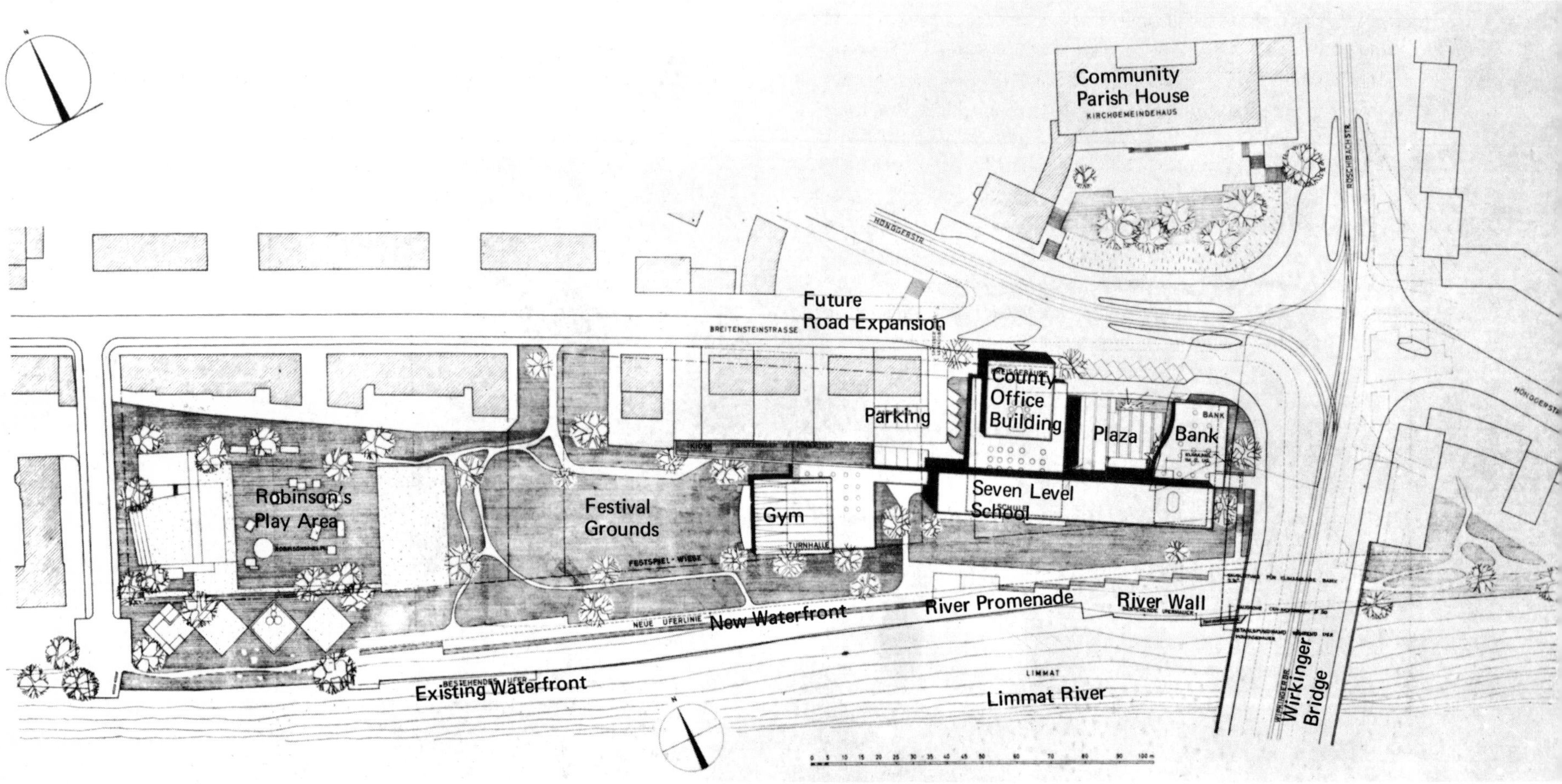

Community
Parish House
KIRCHGEMEINDEHAUS
Future
Road Expansion
BREITENSTEINSTRASSE
HÖNGGERSTR
County
Office
Building
Parking
Plaza
Bank
Robinson's
Play Area
Festival
Grounds
Gym
TURNHALLE
Seven Level
School
FESTSPIEL-WIESE
River Promenade
River Wall
NEUE UFERLINIE
New Waterfront
BESTEHENDES UFER
Existing Waterfront
LIMMAT
Limmat River
Wirkinger
Bridge
N

By public law all governmental, civic, and educational buildings must provide below ground blast shelters with manual air circulation systems and several escape hatches. The plan of the lower floor of the administrative center indicated many such large compartments provided, complete with provisions storage and all in a state of necessary preparedness. Moreover, these rooms have no other purpose, not even storage.

All educational buildings of fair size provide for an on-site caretaker to whom the school delegates the overall security of the structures. All visitors without appointments must make their presence and purpose known to him prior to entering the school proper. A visitors' bell is generally provided somewhere near the main lobby and a few minutes wait will produce a courteous though inquisitive

caretaker. The size of this complex obviously required two such custodians, whose apartments are located atop the county administration building.

When built, the auditorium-gymnasium which we mentioned earlier will serve the school, but it is also intended for community use as well. The same thing is true of the choral classroom, which might in future be used by local singing groups after it has served as the school's singing room during the daytime. Hopefully, this site will at all times be lively and colorful as well as handsome in its setting along the Limmat River. Through their architect's design, the educational and city planners hope to stimulate the entire community's participation in events which will find both pleasant and adequate spaces. The architect for this project was Ernst Schindler, B.S.A.,S.I.A.

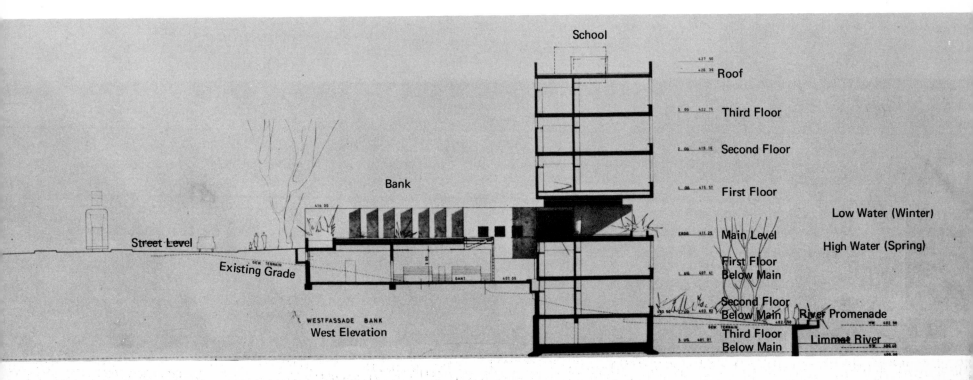

77. 40

26.00 42.00

9. 40 30

4. 20 40

STUTZMAUER MIT EINBAUTEN DARÜBER SCHÜLERGARTEN

Retaining Wall **Gardens above this area**

pissoir

ABSTELLR Q 2 KIOSK Q1 ÜBERDECKTE HALLE WC HERREN Q 4 PUTZ Q5 GARDEROBE Q 6 GARDEROBE Q 7 MAG QUART Q 8 MAGAZIN QUART Q 9
B fl 32 5 1350 402 80 B fl 25.50 B fl 26.30 B fl 27.00 B fl 153.00
1550 25 25 25

Storage 30 **Small Shops**

Covered Passageway

WC DAMEN Q 3 403.82 40

sturzfenster

oberlicht 403.82 ÜBERDECKTER VERBINDUNGSKORRIDOR

S 0023

GARD T 004 PLATTEZIMMER S
B fl 13.00 B fl 64 80
30 F fl 22 85

1.30 1.00 40 T 007 **Iron**
Stage LFHR U SAN T **Room**
B fl 8 50
VORPLATZ T 003 F fl 0.85 WASCHR T 005
B fl 13.80
podium B fl 13.00 GARD T 006

garderobe
B fl 13.00

VORPLATZ T 001
B fl 15 10
F fl 5 50

Auditorium 80 **Gym** PUTZ
Stage T 0010
T 008

KLAV T 0011 T 009 40 16. 80

FESTWIESE 402 70
17. 80

30 25 **Music and**
Choral Room
402 82

Roof Shell

403 82 GERÄTE T 0013 SINGRAAM 140 PL T 002 40
TURNHALLE T 0012 B fl 22 50 B fl 44 00
Festival Grounds B fl 198.00 1.00
F fl 402 50

1.30 40

BUHNE

Building Setback Line
BAULINIE 9. 80 1.40 13. 90

1.30 13.00 11. 80

23.00

BOMB SHELTER CAPACITIES—TOTAL 583

NOTAUSSTIEG

HAUSWIRTSCHAFTLICHE
FORTBILDUNGSSCHULE

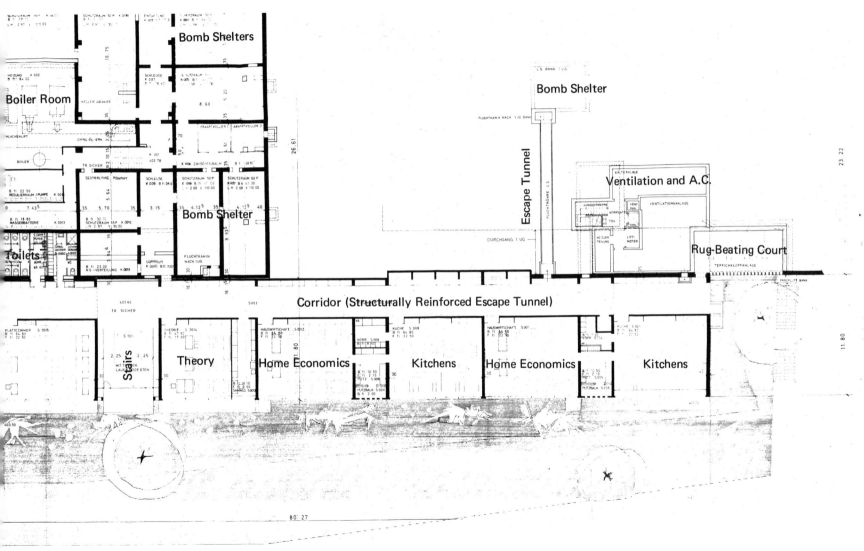

Bomb Shelters

Boiler Room

Bomb Shelter

Ventilation and A.C.

Bomb Shelter

Escape Tunnel

Rug-Beating Court

Toilets

53

Corridor (Structurally Reinforced Escape Tunnel)

Stairs

Theory

Home Economics

Kitchens

Home Economics

Kitchens

Lower Floor

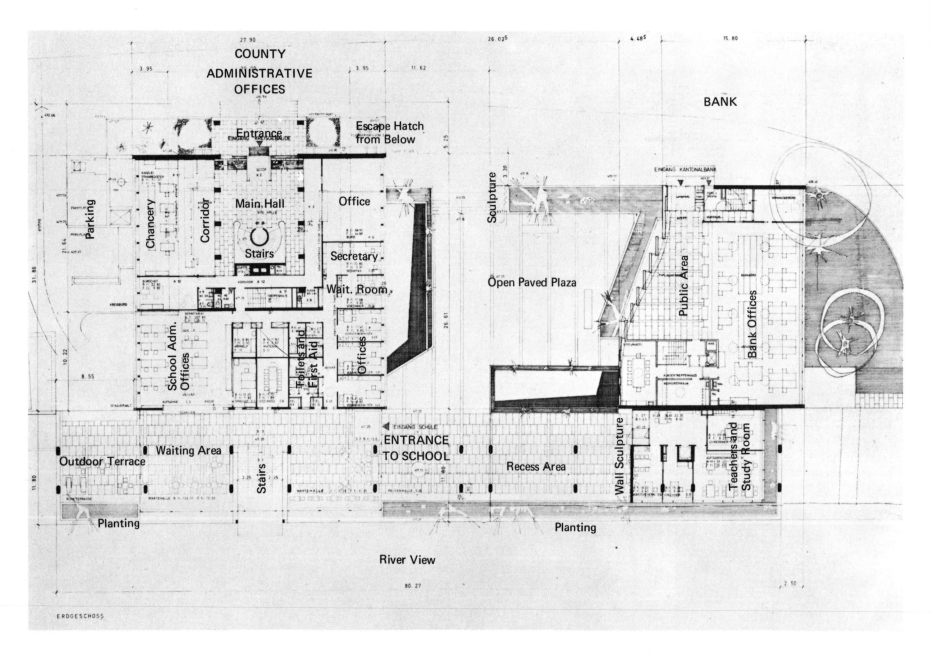

54

COUNTY
ADMINISTRATIVE
OFFICES

BANK

Escape Hatch
from Below

Entrance
EINGANG BÜROGEBÄUDE

Sculpture

Parking

Chancery

Corridor

Main Hall

Office

Open Paved Plaza

Public Area

Bank Offices

EINGANG KANTONALBANK

Stairs

Secretary

Wait. Room

School Adm.
Offices

Toilets and First Aid

Offices

Outdoor Terrace

Waiting Area

Stairs

Planting

ENTRANCE
TO SCHOOL

Recess Area

Wall Sculpture

Teachers and Study Room

Planting

River View

ERDGESCHOSS

**HAUSWIRTSCHAFTLICHE
FORTBILDUNGSSCHULE**

PLAN AT STREET LEVEL

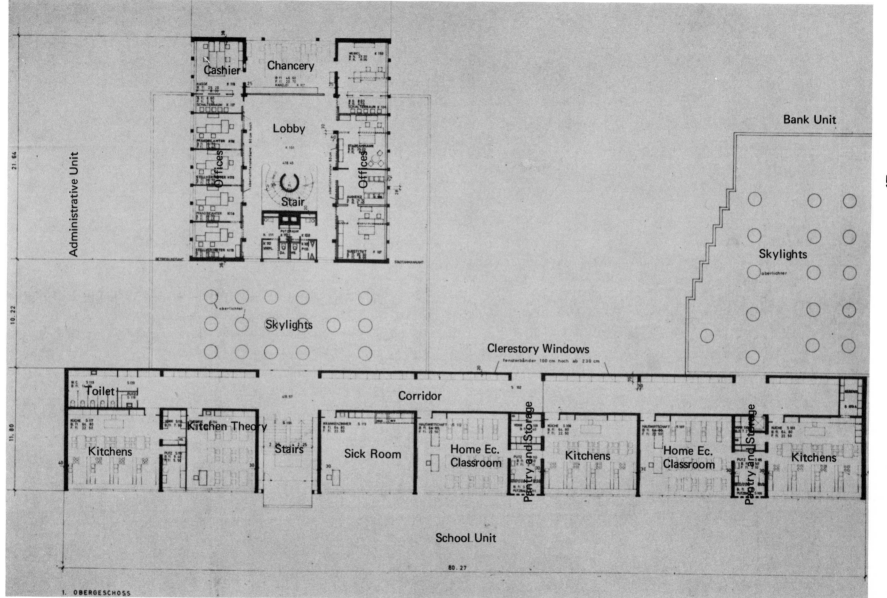

Administrative Unit

Bank Unit

55

Cashier

Chancery

Lobby

Offices

Offices

Stair

Skylights

Skylights

Clerestory Windows

Corridor

Toilet

Kitchen Theory

Stairs

Sick Room

Home Ec. Classroom

Pantry and Storage

Kitchens

Home Ec. Classroom

Pantry and Storage

Kitchens

Kitchens

School Unit

80. 27

1. OBERGESCHOSS

KANTONSSCHULE FREUDENBERG
Zurich, Switzerland

A commercial school for boys housing 800 students and a classical school for 300 boys are combined in this complex. The students are mostly from the southern part of the canton. They are required to maintain a four-point average for acceptance (based on a six-point system), as well as to pass several high level entrance exams.

A common-facilities building houses the auditorium and cafeteria.

The large site provides a soccer field, tennis courts, and car park for instructors. Completely enclosed bicycle halls for students are provided on the lower level. Landscaping is a well thought out design which integrates several natural levels. Large excavated rocks have been used to form rock gardens, and two-story tree wells to preserve many existing trees while providing vistas to levels below. The theatre combines with a stepped amphitheatre which doubles as an outdoor stage for drama and small musical presentations. There is outdoor dining space off the cafeteria. Movable seating arrangements permit the theatre to serve several varied functions from intimate arena style viewing to large orchestration. Adjustable ceiling baffles help to "tune" the theatre for the varied presentations.

Classroom size is based on a working unit of 20 pupils. All rooms have natural light sources, and fluorescent strip lighting is provided on two sides of each classroom as a supplement. Dropped corridor ceilings allow additional clerestory lighting from above the corridor roofs. Of special merit are the large exhibition areas off connecting corridors which provide space for interesting displays in science, chemistry, and biology. Live fish and animals, serviced from the storage area, are frequently exhibited.

A large part of the students' social life centers on this school. There are vocal clubs, music and dance groups, cinema clubs, and other activities, liberally supervised but not regulated by the school administration.

THE SITE

The site adjoins a city park and is heavily wooded and steeply inclined. In European fashion, the architect, Prof. J. Schader, allowed the existing characteristics of the topography to remain by keeping the vegetation and following the hillsite silhouette with his stepped buildings. A wide green belt reduces city noise and hides the traffic as well. Since the theatre and cafeteria are frequently used by local townspeople, the approach to these facilities was made accessible to the public road and parking; other main campus accesses are off quiet streets. Public night school also utilizes the science tract and physical education building. The main quadrangle "core" of the campus was placed at the level top of the hill, and this area was extended to a size of 150 by 80 meters by using the low element roofs as pedestrian ramps at the corresponding level of the higher grade.

The large open lobby area (complete with ornamental water fountains under the stairways), which opens to the exterior by sliding glass doors, serves as versatile display space for art, science exhibitions, craft work, etc. Student activities groups hold meetings here in off school hours, and community functions are frequently accommodated.

The accompanying cross sections illustrate the cross ventilation and day lighting the European architect utilizes in his classroom design. This effect is not only desired by local educational and student groups but required by Swiss law, and thus orientation is highly crucial in site planning.

Of particular merit is the special treatment of plant and live animal displays in science tract corridors. Rather than relegated to dead storage, the entire collection of science teaching-aids remains educational—even when not being used in classroom instruction. The full length glass cases occur between the material storage rooms and the corridors and serve to identify the divisions of biology, zoology, or botany through which the student moves. This adds increased interest to the chore of circulation while visually expanding the traffic zone.

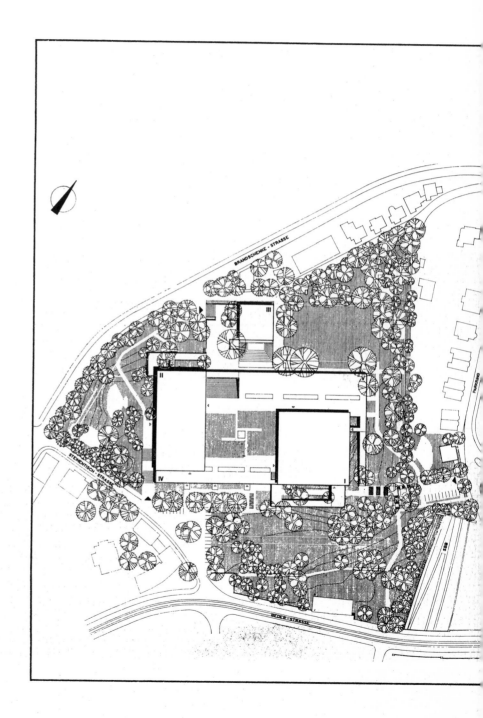

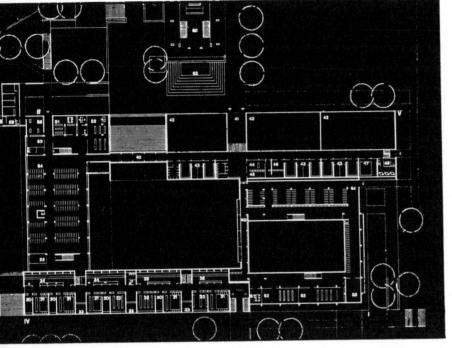

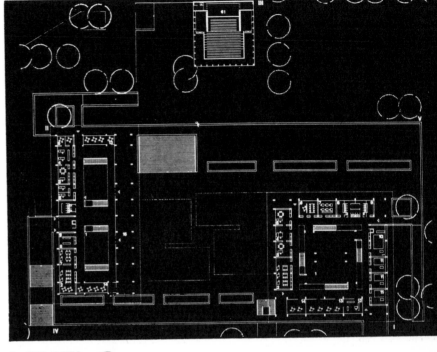

LEVEL 1   ## LEVEL 2

KEY:

I   Academic Highschool
II Commercial Highschool
1. Ground Floor Hall
2. Teacher's Preparation Area
3. Principal's Office
4. Administrative Office
5. Asst. Principal's Office
6. Conference Room

7. Teachers' Library
8. Teachers' Wardrobe
9. Receptionist
10. History Classroom
11. Special Purpose Classroom
12. Students' Library
13. Students' Reading Room
14. Students' Preparation Room

15. Covered Recess Hall
16. Classrooms
17. Sketching Class
18. Model Room
19. Geometric Sketching Class
20. Typing Class
21. Office
22. Library for commercial subjects

23. Hallway
24. Terrace
51. Meeting Room for
    Students' Organizations
52. Library
53. Storage
54. Bicycle Racks
55. Craft Room
56. Caretaker's Apartment

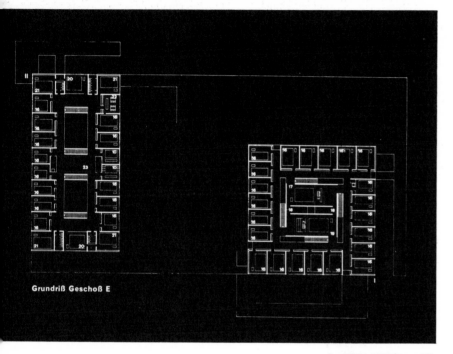

Grundriß Geschoß E

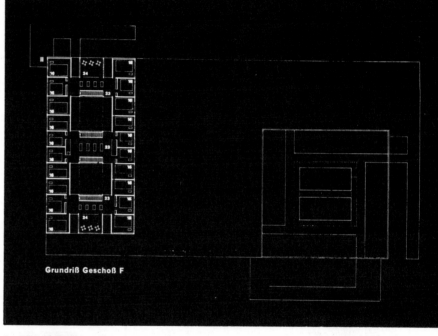

Grundriß Geschoß F

LEVEL 3   LEVEL 4

IV SCIENCE TRACT
30. Preparation
31. Auditorium
32. Science Lab
33. Bomb Shelter Entrance
34. Geography Collection
35. Biology Collection

V PHYSICAL EDUCATION FACILITIES
40. Connecting Hallway to Students' Locker Area
41. Entry
42. Gymnastics Rooms
43. Lockers and Showers

44. Receptionist
45. Central Wardrobe for Outside Organizations
46. First-Aid Room
47. Physical Theory Room
48. Physical Education Teacher and Wardrobe

III AUDITORIUM
60. Entry
61. Theatre with Stage
62. Amphitheatre
63. Cafeteria

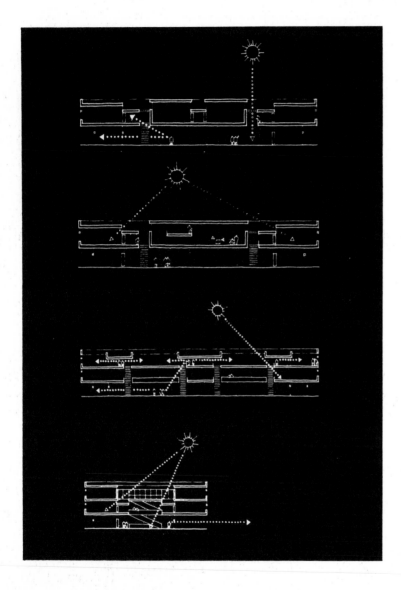

There are three fully equipped gymnastic rooms for body training exercises.

Faculty rooms include offices, storage lockers in natural wood, a library, and coffee and smoking rooms, with hot plates provided to prepare small snacks.

The eleven and one-half acre site was purchased by the canton in a central city location as early as 1948, at the cost of 5.8 million Swiss franks (1⅓ million dollars). An educational program was developed in 1953 and the following year an architectural competition was held, and with minor modifications the successful scheme was adopted. A public referendum in 1956 approved the winning plan at a cost of 26,000,000 S.F. (nearly 6 million dollars) and construction began that year. The first sections of the facility were opened in 1959, and on May 26, 1961, the entire complex was dedicated.

Good design rarely goes unnoticed in Switzerland; this project, however, was also awarded international acclaim at the São Paulo Bienal in 1961.

The educational program called for two schools on one campus with several jointly used facilities:

A. An <u>OBERREALSCHULE</u> (classical school) giving boys between the ages of 10 and 19 university preparation courses.
B. A <u>HANDELSSCHULE</u> (commercial high school) giving both the Matura and Diplom certificates, also for boys between 10 and 19.
C. Common usage facilities consisting of a 500 seat theatre, an 80 place cafeteria, a science tract, and three physical education areas.

THE AUDITORIUM

One of the most interesting features of the campus is the multi-faceted theatre building—the "focal-point" of the entire complex. This combination concert hall, community center, and flexible theatre is capable of total blackout for audio-visual presentation or completely open viewing.

The versatility of the non-oriented theatre arrangement and corresponding acoustical adjustability illustrates the conceptual approach used in its design, namely a hall for varied and resourceful experiences rather than conventional one type presentation. This space has been effectively used in six different "variations" as shown in the accompanying plans and sections:

1. Conventional proscenium with single or three sided spectator seating, traditionally effective for the play form with simple backdrops. Lectures or musical presentations usually require this form.
2. Expanded stage wing without side audience, this form is used for the larger stage area required by modern dance or ballet and can be obtained by moving the proscenium walls backward.
3. Three part stage with wings used for either modern drama or dance presentation where surrounding the audience is particularly effective.
4. Theatre in the round for the four sided spectator viewing required of the intimate arena staging.
5. Reverse step staging with performers elevated. In this form simple backdrops can be set up on the higher level platform while the audience seating can be tiered on the conventional stage end.
6. The night club arrangement illustrates the extreme of versatility and this setup is utilized to accommodate the formal dances and "proms" occuring throughout the school year.

It will be noted that lighting, nonfixed seating, and acoustical baffling are all totally adaptable to any of the above conditions without expensive and complicated underfloor machinery, and any of these arrangements can be changed with a minimum expenditure of labor. Nor are the above arrangements necessarily the limits of possibility; the "thrust-stage," for instance, could work with several of the above forms.

In proximity to this theater are the cafeteria, kitchen, and outdoor amphitheatre. Refreshments can be served to patrons of either theatre and tables are set onto the amphitheatre floor or on the overhead terrace. This amphitheatre becomes an informal student meeting area and frequently impromptu musical groups will assemble to perform for fellow classmates.

FLEXIBLE USE OF THE AUDITORIUM:

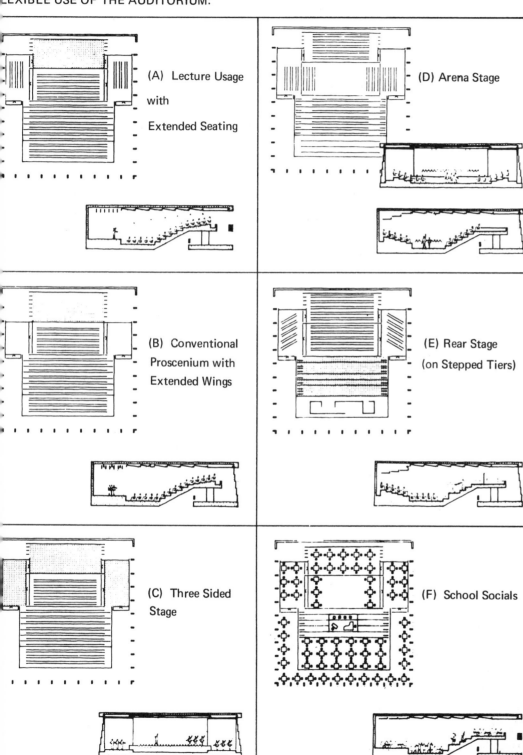

(A) Lecture Usage with Extended Seating

(B) Conventional Proscenium with Extended Wings

(C) Three Sided Stage

(D) Arena Stage

(E) Rear Stage (on Stepped Tiers)

(F) School Socials

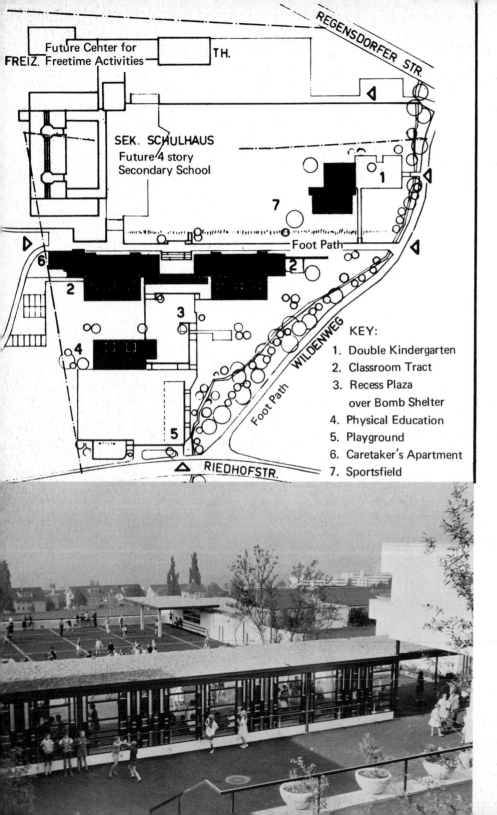

KEY:
1. Double Kindergarten
2. Classroom Tract
3. Recess Plaza
   over Bomb Shelter
4. Physical Education
5. Playground
6. Caretaker's Apartment
7. Sportsfield

RIEDHOF SCHOOL
Zurich, Switzerland

Although the term "educational park" is unfamiliar as such to educational planners in Europe, they nevertheless are convinced the multiple school facility in a landscaped environment holds the key to many educational "ills." The first two increments of this kindergarten-through-secondary facility have recently been completed on a compact hillside site overlooking woods and valleys high above the distracting noise of city traffic. The double kindergarten occupies the upper terrace and is deliberately separated from the two elementary school tracts, accessible by pedestrian paths only. The interiors are cheerful with busy displays of children's exhibits and a large indoor play area.

The elementary school has been divided into two groups of 225 students, each occupying a separate structure but joined by a 12 x 95 foot recess hall gaily embellished with colored glass inserts and open on the courtyard side, providing an effective windbreak and link between buildings. Each unit has its own multipurpose areas for group indoor activities, but whenever possible outdoor instruction is conducted on the courtyards adjoining these rooms. Other terraces are generously used on lower planes of the site down to the physical educational facilities with the related exercise playfields, strategically placed to reduce the noise levels at the academic classrooms. A large bomb shelter occupies the area under the recess plaza with its equipped community first aid rooms.

The interiors rely on natural wood paneling and drapery rather than tile or venetian blinds to avoid effectively the institutional look, and the architect took pains to give the project his personal touch in the specially designed vinyl floor patterns and sculptured exterior ground lighting fixtures. Landscaping has been handled with great sensitivity and recognition of its intrinsic value to the total scheme. The architect for this project was Prof. Alfred Roth, B.S.A., S.I.A.

COST DATA	SWISS FRANC	$ U.S. (approx.) = 4.36 S.F.
Land and road construction	2, 307, 000	$ 530,000
Building construction	2, 321, 000	533,000
Landscaping and sitework	592, 200	136,000
Bomb shelter	495, 000	114,000
Furnishings	334, 000	77,000
Miscellaneous	180, 000	41,000
TOTAL	6, 230, 000	$1,431,000

HAMBVRGVM.

DIE E...

FLVV...

DER
ALSTER

HAMBURG

9. Alte Gran.
10. Die Bewrs.
11. S. Niclaus.
12. Hopfe marckt.
1. Pferdt marckt.   13. Der News Gran.
2. Opn borge.   14. Heileg Geyst.
3. S. Peter.   15. Ballestal.
4. Der Domb.   16. S. Maria Magdalena.
5. S. Iacob.   17. S. Iohann.
6. S. Gertraud.   18. Weisenhause.
7. Fyschmark.   19. Rathause.
8. S. Caterina.   20. Zur Schuise.

5

HANSESTADT HAMBURG, an original member of the Hanseatic League of "free trade" city ports, has a long history of self-government as a "city-state" independent of any control other than the national government. Today, the city is one of the thirteen independent states of the new Republic of Germany and, as such, its school bureau (Hamburger Hochbauamt) is autonomous, as opposed to the rest of Germany where the schools are governed by the local state laws.

War damage in the downtown area of Hamburg was approximated at 70 percent as compared to 20 percent in the suburbs. It is, therefore, understandable why school building is invariably related to city planning or urban renewal and, indeed, these total community complexes are among the most impressive contributions Hamburg is making in contemporary social philosophy. One such development, ALTONA KÖNIGSTRASSE, is described later in this section. Moreover, almost one half of the school buildings in use in 1939 were either totally destroyed or received such extensive damage that they were inoperable at war's end. Conventional school building methods were augmented by prefabricated component systems, and although these were used extensively all over the city, they are undeniably considered an emergency measure by both the school bureau as well as the citizenry. Nevertheless, we were shown two types of precast wall units worthy of mention in the following pages.

The accompanying chart illustrates the main flow of the German educational system. It must be borne in mind, however, that the student has many alternatives which have the effect of "hand-tailoring" the education to his needs, especially at the vocational level.

German education, like its counterparts all over Europe, is in a state of flux. Postwar commercial development has been rapid, indeed so rapid that the Germans, with characteristic fondness for nicknames, refer to themselves as "wir Wunderkinder." Germany's supply of technical talent to the common market has produced increased demand on its educational system and the legendary rigidness of former years is yielding to the broader demands of the new generation. Addressing ourselves to this problem while in Hamburg, we reviewed the vocational school patterns and found them to be among the most specialized in Europe.

There are over 40 different types of vocational schools in Hamburg, ranging from the extensively equipped engineering trades to the simplest occupation. A walk through the city streets will easily demonstrate the specialized training given to those who choose window dressing, counter sales, or table waiting as their vocation. Such occupations are not considered menial and temporary pursuits that need no adequate preparation; rather, such tasks are given an enriched status and a high degree of competent performance through proper schooling. The German educational philosophy considers this an integral part of its role and the public servants try to maintain the standards.

Usually these technical schools are attended for eight hours per week on a single day. The students range in age from 15 to 19 years but the majority continue without interruption from Volksschule. By German law, vocational students must go to these schools for three years while they maintain related jobs in their field. The employers are required to release them weekly for this training, for which they receive no pay, although they are paid set scale wages by the employer for the days they do work. The schooling is, of course, free except for small sums necessary to buy study materials. Adults frequently attend these classes for purposes of refresher courses, retraining, or personal enjoyment. Night school is very popular with adults and frequently the courses have as heavy a load in the evening as in the daytime. Special "Fachschulen" are designated for adult purposes and the courses are modified for older citizens.

The school retains the products of the students' work, frequently exhibiting them in displays within the school or in the downtown area. The public may buy these items from the school at appropriate prices and the school purchases additional materials from the proceeds.

There is a trend toward giving complete work experience in the schools for the full 3 year program, thereby eliminating cooperative work experience outside the school. This would enable the school to broaden the educational exposure of the student and reduce the high degree of specialization—a result of the present system however competent the worker becomes in his craft. Upon completion of the three year apprenticeship, the student takes an examination that rates theoretical and academic understanding as well as technical accomplishment. Frequently, as in the cabinetmaker's school, the student must design and execute a "Meisterstück" which is carefully rated by the craftmasters of the school. Only then does the student receive the coveted certificate. (The quality of student work that we saw submitted exceeded that of their commercial counterparts.)

University training occurs on a level removed from vocational education and, therefore, the university that comprises only the classical faculties enjoys a unique prestige of scholarship in the country.

Physical education is handled differently in Europe than in the United States, and since this affects site appropriations and has a direct bearing on the way schools are designed, it is worthy of some attention.

For every 700 children an increment of 1.8 hectares (approximately 4½ acres of land is considered necessary for a school site. Approximately 40 percent of this is used for physical education. As in London, larger playfield sites are maintained outside the downtown area and students are transported for large field play. Field houses or "Turnhallen" are constructed, usually as separate structures, along prototype lines (120 of these in Hamburg follow a design by Paul Seitz) and are mainly equipped with gymnastic apparatus. Periods of "free play" (i.e. basketball) are discouraged in favor of medically oriented body-building exercise. Team play and professionalism in spectator sports is considered too limiting by the carefully-trained gymnastic instructors, who concentrate on muscular coordination and a balanced development of the bone structure. Swimming occupies an increasingly important role in German physical education, especially in the younger grades, where instruction begins at age 6 or 7 and is given for one or more hours per week. There are plans to build 40 pools in elementary schools of the Hamburg area; five were completed at the time of this survey. These pools are 25 x 50 x 4½ feet deep, with one side stepped for swimming instruction.

Students may use the local sports clubs or "Turnverein," which provide facilities for graded sports activities. For a nominal fee adults may also utilize these institutions. The enthusiasm for physical fitness is usually well enough grounded in the student that he continues to be athletically active throughout his life. This accounts for the popularity of the athletic clubs throughout the nation, and, if a young man decides to become a professional athlete, it is here rather than in the school system that these abilities are fostered and subsidized. Professional athletics of the spectator variety such as soccer are very popular in Germany.

AGE OF STUDENT	THE SCHOOL SYSTEM IN HAMBURG, GERMANY			SCHOOL GRADE		
19 +	PROFESSIONAL – TECHNICAL WITH APPRENTICESHIPS (FACHSCHULE)	UNIVERSITY (HOCHSCHULE)				
18 – 19	(BERUFSSCHULE – BERUFSFACHSCHULE)	SECONDARY SCHOOL (Gymnasium)	Commercial High School (Wirtschafts- Gymnasium)	13		HIGHER STUDIES
17 – 18	(BERUFSSCHULE – BERUFSFACHSCHULE)	SECONDARY SCHOOL (Gymnasium)		12		HIGHER STUDIES
16 – 17	(BERUFSSCHULE – BERUFSFACHSCHULE)	SECONDARY SCHOOL (Gymnasium)		11		HIGHER STUDIES
15 – 16	(BERUFSSCHULE – BERUFSFACHSCHULE)	SECONDARY SCHOOL (Gymnasium)		10		HIGHER STUDIES
14 – 15	UPPER ELEMENTARY (OBERSTUFE)	MIDDLE SCHOOL (MITTLESCHULE)	SECONDARY SCHOOL (Gymnasium)	9		COMPULSORY EDUCATION
13 – 14	UPPER ELEMENTARY (OBERSTUFE)		SECONDARY SCHOOL (Gymnasium)	8		COMPULSORY EDUCATION
12 – 13	UPPER ELEMENTARY (OBERSTUFE)		SECONDARY SCHOOL (Gymnasium)	7		COMPULSORY EDUCATION
11 – 12	MIDDLE ELEMENTARY		SECONDARY SCHOOL (Gymnasium)	6	RETARDED CHILDREN (non-graded)	COMPULSORY EDUCATION
10 – 11	MIDDLE ELEMENTARY		SECONDARY SCHOOL (Gymnasium)	5	RETARDED CHILDREN (non-graded)	ELEMENTARY (VOLKSCHULE)
9 – 10	LOWER ELEMENTARY (GRUNDSCHULE)			4		ELEMENTARY (VOLKSCHULE)
8 – 9	LOWER ELEMENTARY (GRUNDSCHULE)			3		ELEMENTARY (VOLKSCHULE)
7 – 8	LOWER ELEMENTARY (GRUNDSCHULE)			2		ELEMENTARY (VOLKSCHULE)
6 – 7	LOWER ELEMENTARY (GRUNDSCHULE)			1		ELEMENTARY (VOLKSCHULE)
4 – 6	KINDERGARTEN (OPTIONAL)			K		

ALTONA KÖNIGSTRASSE
Hamburg, Germany

Altona, an industrial area of Hamburg, was hard hit in World War II due to its importance as a main harbor port. This particular residential area was almost totally destroyed and subsequently was acquired by the school bureau as a future school site. School programming officials determined that two "Volksschulen" were necessary in this area of the city, each to accommodate 700 students in twenty classrooms. According to Hamburg formula, 1400 students between the ages of 6 to 15 years would require 3.6 hectares of land, including recreational space; however, this ample site measured 105 x 500 meters or roughly 10 acres of urban Hamburg real estate.

A problem of major importance to postwar Germany, perhaps rivaling that of educational planning for rising birth rates, is the care and attention of older citizens, many of whom were left unattended at war's end. Here was an opportunity to utilize a large site for a two-fold purpose, and so a community center came into the planning considerations, related to, yet independent from, the double school facility.

A 300 seat auditorium is planned to accommodate school and public events, with a small music room adjoining for choral and instrumental workshops. A "home of the open door," a youth canteen facility, will provide after-hours space for dancing, hobbies, crafts, or special projects, and will be in daily operation from 6 to 10 P.M. Special workshops, science laboratories, art rooms, metal and wood-working shops are intended for student academic use by day and adult hobby use by night, with trained instructors present on an advisory basis. The gymnastics building will be student oriented during the school day and available for adult "physical fitness" in the evenings, and since Germans are natural enthusiasts for exercise, ample participation in this program is anticipated. Perhaps one of the most unique combinations being attempted here is the construction of club rooms and social centers for use specifically by the elderly on a day and night basis. The poignant presence of the elderly generation within a school site seems a most interesting social experiment. There will also be a pre-school playground for small tots taking an afternoon "bummel" with their mothers.

At this writing approximately half of the facility is in operation with the remainder scheduled for construction shortly. The cruciform classroom buildings contain ten classrooms each, two on the ground floor with administrative areas, small library, and lounge, and four classrooms on the second and third floors around a central open stairwell. The classrooms and the physical education buildings are constructed entirely from prefabricated concrete structural frame components with brick veneers. Many of these structures, along with their modern counterpart, the hexagonal "beehive" component, have been built throughout the city. The architect for this complex was Paul Seitz, Dipl. Arch.

Is this type of school, combined with the social center approach as programmed at Altona, a unique one-time solution or a prototype of educational thinking in Germany? "We'll wait and see," declare Hamburg officials.

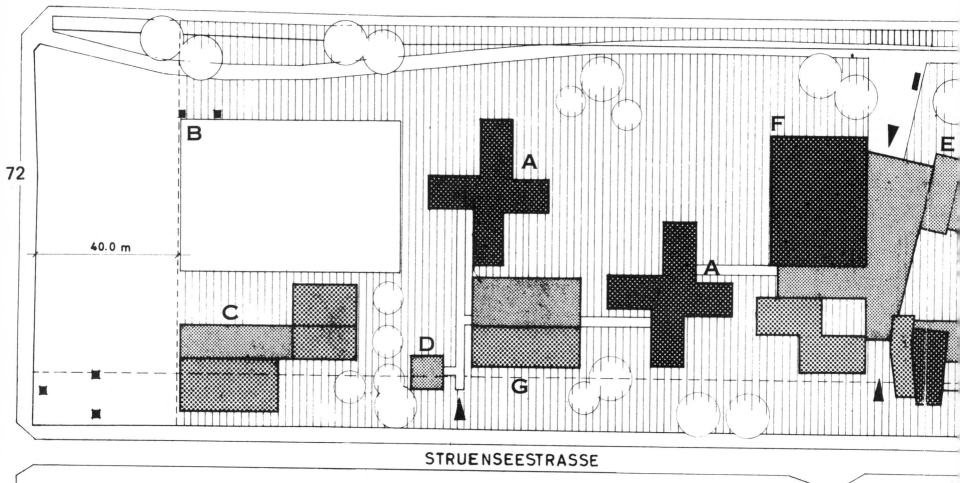

KÖNIGSTRASSE

72

40.0 m

B

C

D

A

A

G

F

E

STRUENSEESTRASSE

A — CLASSROOM UNITS
B — SPORTS FIELD
C — FIELD HOUSE
D — CARETAKER'S FLAT
E — STUDENT SOCIAL HALL
AND WORKROOMS

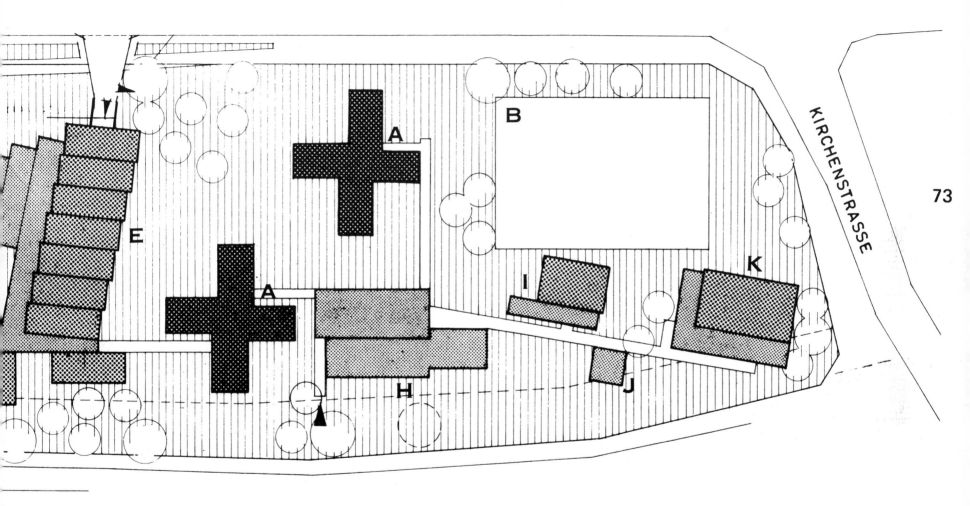

F — CLUB FOR ELDERLY
G — MUSIC HALL
H — ADMINISTRATION
I — GYMNASTICS
J — RESIDENCE FOR ADMINISTRATOR
K — FIELD HOUSE (FUTURE)

FIRST PHASE

ULTIMATE PLAN

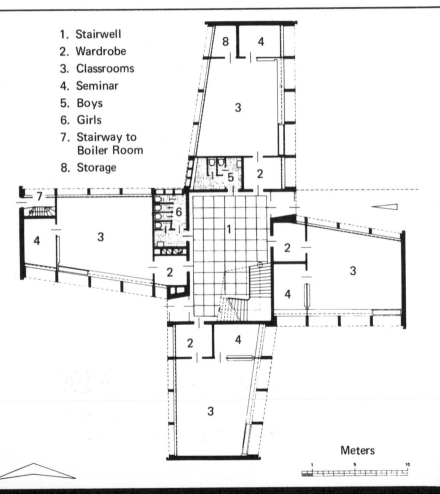

1. Stairwell
2. Wardrobe
3. Classrooms
4. Seminar
5. Boys
6. Girls
7. Stairway to Boiler Room
8. Storage

Meters

ALTONA KÖNIGSTRASSE

TYPICAL CLASSROOM UNIT

"SCHOOLS IN THE GREEN"
Educational Landscaping in Hamburg

The recreation area for today's city youth is constantly being diminished; in all too many urban areas it is nonexistent. Economic "progress," housing needs for the ever increasing population, and the voracious demands of the automobile have all contributed to the systematic elimination of green spaces within the city; moreover, construction of new playgrounds, parks, and sports fields has in no way compensated for these losses. Educators in Hamburg feel the only effective remedy to this problem lies in the area of new school construction.

We are all aware of the progressive outlines for landscaping given in national and international conferences on school planning, guidelines supported by educational and health agencies. We are also aware that even so there have been limited achievements of any high quality.

Eighteen years ago, recognizing the value of landscaping-with-architecture as an indivisible unity in the educational process, Hamburg initiated a pilot program to set school buildings amid green areas. Moreover, to realize maximum value of such an expenditure for the children, the school and its grounds would be accessible beyond the actual hours of the class program. It was hoped that this would satisfy the child's need to share in the "ownership" of an area expressly intended for him. The program was initiated with certain standards for site development, where possible in conformity with internationally agreed upon guidelines. The following requirements are set forth in Hamburg's "Official Building Program for School Grounds":

1. For a school of twenty classrooms (circa 650-700 students), an area of 18,000 M^2 (190,000 square feet) would be required including intermission courtyards and gardens.
2. A physical education area of 7,000 M^2 (75,000 square feet) in addition to the above.

These requirements indicate a need for 35 M^2 (375 square feet) per student. However, it is not so much the amount of ground allotted as what is accomplished with this space in Hamburg. The architect nearly always coordinates with a landscape architect for the sake of integrating this vital aspect of site planning.

Wilhelm Dressler, head director of schools for Hamburg, has written the following in a recent publication of "Garten und Landschaft": "The inner reason for new school architecture lies ultimately in the use of standards and needs derived directly from the growing child. Complementary to the home, the schools should be a haven for youth where they enjoy being and where they find an atmosphere that creates a good foundation for academic and educational work. Instead of the huge, multi-storied building that represents a mammoth and impersonal complex, there are today small units placed in useful arrangement. They are easier for the student to understand and create a home-like feeling with their light and friendly rooms. The entire complex is imbedded and surrounded by green areas so that the school now presents itself as an organically membered and landscaped unity. Thus, the building type of the "School in the Green" is created as a modern school organism where all parts have their place and reason within the entity."

The following photographs illustrate clearly Mr. Dressler's intention. Landscape, like any other tool of education, is a part of the learning process, and as such is budgeted as an integral and indispensable item of contract—never an afterthought or of unprofessional concern. Children are taught values of animal and plant life with biological sciences in their own personal areas. Vandalism to items of landscape is virtually nonexistent. Quite to the contrary, children are urged to tend their gardens and aquariums with loving care, frequently doing so after normal school hours. For them school is always open and the social center of activity. A sense of pride in ownership being thus achieved, vandalism is pointless.

BINDFELDWEG

"ART IN ARCHITECTURE"...A BUDGETARY ALLOWANCE

The plan arrangement of the individual building follows a general principle. The classrooms of the lower grades together with the small gym and the recess courtyard from one grouping. The intermediate and upper grades, the large gym and recess courtyard, and the tract of special classrooms form the second grouping, while administration, community hall, music hall, and central recess hall form the combining link that unites the entire complex.

The playgrounds are arranged so that exercise activities do not disturb the teaching in the classrooms. Since European architects and educators reject windowless classrooms, these are all oriented for natural exposure and are arranged so that, wherever possible, views open on to garden courts while recess courtyards lie toward the rear of the complex. Similarly, classroom windows always occur on two sides for natural ventilation; air conditioning is not utilized and only moderate reliance on audio-visual techniques makes blackout requirements unnecessary to any extent. Instead, the schools frequently utilize educational radio programs.

We observed that heavy maintenance on the lawns and landscape was very good in most cases and is generally financed by the city.

It should be obvious even to the casual observer that what is represented by a "school in the green" is not merely a nice area of lawn with the usual groupings of trees and indiscriminate bushes scattered around, but the carefully thought out fulfillment of an educational concept. A case in point is the natural science gardens where plant groupings are carefully coordinated with fields of botanical study or the related terrariums and fish ponds of biological interest to the student. The daily communication with everything that grows or blooms in these gardens, whether experienced during outdoor class lessons or recess periods or even after school hours, becomes an important educational experience especially for the child of the city.

In addition, a budgetary allowance for "art-in-architecture" of between one and two percent of the total construction costs enables the architect to enrich the total environment with appropriate outdoor sculpture or mosaic work. The child thus comes into contact early in his formative years with well chosen examples of artistic expression, sparing him the later shock and rejection through ridicule typical of the unexposed and insensitive adult.

It was not intended that the garden and park services of Hamburg would alone be responsible for the maintenance of each school's landscape, although to them falls the responsibility for the heavy or complicated work: the school itself must participate in the upkeep of its grounds. More specifically it is to the children that the care and responsibility is delegated and, supplied with appropriate tools, guidebooks, and encouragement, they respond readily, not only in the lower grades but throughout their school life. Annual garden competitions between neighboring and intra-city schools engender as much student enthusiasm as our own Thanksgiving Day football tussles with the big rival. The Municipality inspects each school and winning groups are given additional funds for landscape items, the grand prize usually being a valuable painting for the school lobby. Not surprisingly, there is no lack of young volunteer horticulturists to care for the gardens during weekends and summer vacations. Garden or building vandalism is virtually non-existent, since the "institution" alone would not sustain the loss. The child who plants a flower is not likely to destroy it.

For the neighbors of these schools the well-kept grounds are a valuable contribution to the cityscape, and for the city's educators and architects, an obligation toward the youth, contributing to his richer school experience, has not been overlooked—such an opportunity once missed may be lost forever, or to paraphrase appropriately from Goethe, "It is not enough to want, it must also be done."

Blankenese

Kirchenweg

Kirchenw

Blankenes

Kirchenweg

Hermann

SÜLLDORFER KIRCHENWEG
Location: Hamburg, Germany

School:	High School for Girls
Client:	City of Hamburg
Design:	Department for Building, div. school construction
Design of open spaces:	Department for Building, div. garden open spaces: 28,500 sq. meters
Costs:	250,000 DM ($62,500) (site work and landscape only)

This school is situated in Sülldorf, north of the city center of Hamburg-Blankenese. It was erected on a gently sloping site with grade differences of 4 to 5 meters.

The islands of planting within the pavement of the recess courtyards are filled with roses, decorative grasses, specimen shrubs, and other planting. Concrete slabs with slightly differing coloring were used for the pavement of the courtyard.

The total site is fenced in by high bushes of local origin. An old sand pit was converted into the amphitheatre and the steps are solidified only by grass sod.

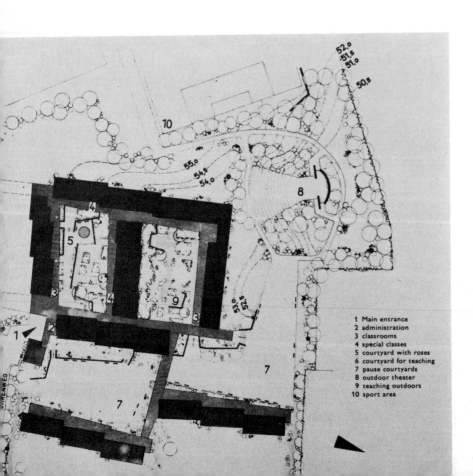

1 Main entrance
2 administration
3 classrooms
4 special classes
5 courtyard with roses
6 courtyard for teaching
7 pause courtyards
8 outdoor theater
9 teaching outdoors
10 sport area

THE GOLBACH VALLEY

Hamburg, Germany

Client: City of Hamburg
Design: City of Hamburg Planning office—div. of school con-
            struction
Site design: Local office Hamburg—dept. of gardens

Legend:
1. Public common green
2. Student youth center
3. Special school for handicapped children
4. Children's day home and nurseries
5. Children's playground
6. Old mill pond
7. Open air swimming pool
8. Public sports field
9. Large elementary school
10. Private club sports field
11. Artificial pond
12. Little brook
13. Old village center (restored)
14. Private rental garden plots for city people (350 m^2 each)

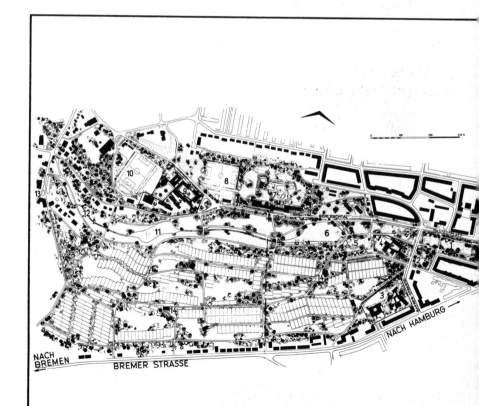

STOCKHOLM

STOCKHOLM

Few countries in the world have achieved Sweden's marriage of architecture and city planning. School building is rarely treated as an entity unto itself but is related to its next larger element—the neighborhood. Swedish architects have also kept the young and the elderly well in mind in the design of their playgrounds and homes for the aged.

Stockholm itself enjoys the unique position of having in its possession vast amounts of unspoiled, undeveloped land adjacent to the city—the rewards of a foresighted land acquisition policy initiated at the turn of the century. Its future expansion possibilities look bright, evident in the relative lack of concern over procurement of suitable school building sites.

A city of less than a half million people in 1918, Stockholm has doubled in size since that time. The recent regional plan of greater Stockholm predicts a future population of one and one half million inhabitants.

Geographically, Stockholm is a most interesting city lying in a wooded archipelago with huge outcroppings of granite.

The city's northern location accounts for its short winter days and long summer ones. Its populated areas have developed equally on either side of a main east-west waterway.

In accordance with master plan provisions, Stockholm is divided into five sections, each with its own cultural, business, and economic center. The suburb sections are programmed at 15,000 inhabitants, each connected to the inner-town district and to each other by a modern underground railway system. Stockholm also has one of the highest automobile concentrations in Europe; it is estimated that one out of every six Swedish inhabitants now owns an automobile.

THE EDUCATIONAL SYSTEM

"GRUNDSKOLAN," the new comprehensive school program now being introduced in Sweden, will be a reality by 1973. A gradual implementation of educational reforms was outlined by the 1961 Parliament and is now in its initial stages. At that time nine years of compulsory attendance at school was programmed for all children. The system will comprise three departments: lower (grades 1-3), middle (grades 4-6), and upper (grades 7-9).

Unlike Switzerland, division within the curriculum does not occur until children reach the upper department; up to that point all pupils study the same subjects and all students in a class are taught by the same instructor.

When a student passes to upper school a certain number of optional subjects are provided that go beyond the common nucleus of subjects and that represent the first deviation from the programmed curriculum. Sweden, like all progressive countries, has a tendency toward a longer school day as well as extended school life; concurrently, there is a trend toward smaller class units of instruction, approximately 25 pupils in the lower department and 30 pupils in grades 4 to 9. When these numbers are exceeded, new classes are formed.

Seven years is the entrance age for most Swedish children into the three grades of the lower department. The first years find the students attending 20 class periods per week. This is gradually increased to 30 by the third year. Stress is placed upon the Swedish language, arithmetic, religion, local history, music, handicraft, and gymnastics.

While infant-school teachers are in charge of instruction in the lower department, the middle department is taught by elementary school teachers; in both departments each class has its own teacher. Special teachers are usually in charge of the practical subjects such as handicrafts, sciences, and gymnastic training. Instruction in the first foreign language (English) begins in grade four and consists of two periods per week divided into four short lessons.

In the middle department both boys and girls receive instruction in textile, wood and metal work—twenty periods per term in each branch of handicraft. There is an endeavor to coordinate the different subjects. The number of weekly periods varies for the middle department, but in general remains about thirty-four. Optional subjects are given beginning with the seventh year.

The upper department is constructed around a curriculum with elected subject material, and it is at this level that defined lines of study emerge, based on a common nucleus of subjects. Students and their parents annually choose subjects for the succeeding year within the elective limits of each program; the educational path thus has many opportunities for early correction depending on the emerging interests and abilities of the student. The advantages of this over a rigid "track system" is immediately apparent. It would appear that this short period of trial and experimentation prior to such an important selection of study is advantageous.

In grade eight students make their selections for the fields of study they will follow from the ninth grade on, and classes are separated by subject area at this point. Parents, in collaboration with their children, decide the subjects to be studied. While the school does not interfere with these selections, it naturally provides necessary information and guidance. Experience has shown that this principle of free choice works rather well, but the responsibility and intelligence of the parents must be correspondingly high. In summary, a unified class group is carried through lower and middle departments not to be split up until the upper department, and only

then to free selection of course material by parents and children with teacher consultation. Subject material can also be further broken down by the relative interest of a student in each subject: it is possible for a pupil to elect an advanced course in mathematics while taking a slower one in English and thereby regulate the degree of intensity in which he matriculates in certain areas. Swedish school officials feel differences between pupils with reference to interests cannot be observed clearly until the age of 15 years. This is one of the reasons why "streaming" is not begun until grade nine. Previous attempts at free selection earlier in the student's career have proved unsuccessful.

Other studies in Sweden seem to indicate that the division of the brighter pupils into special classes at too early an age does not lead to any marked advantage for the bright students but to disadvantages for the others. Rather, the benefits of social cooperation between different individuals and groups in unified instruction outweighs any academic rewards in this age group. All pupils, regardless of their chosen study in the new comprehensive school, must take part in so-called "practical-vocational" guidance. This means that they will spend three weeks during grade 9 at different places of work to gain some experience with various occupations, thereby achieving more insight into vocational trades. Before this occurs students receive theoretical study and vocational orientation in the classroom.

In general outline form the elective "streams" available in grade nine are as follows:

1. Social: High concentration of educational courses.
2. Technical-mechanical: The trade school equivalent.
3. Economics: Business training for management positions.
4. Theoretical: Leading to higher academic training at the University.

In all but the theoretical program students may choose between a very academic approach or a more practical training, depending, for instance, on whether he intends to become a design engineer or a mechanic within the trade.

Continuation Schools for study beyond, and in conjunction with, this nine-year program are not rigidly defined at the time of this writing. (First pupils terminating their studies within the comprehensive plan required these facilities in the fall of 1965.) These, unlike the comprehensive school, will be free of written examinations and rated reports of students' progress. The following diagram may be useful in clarifying the new Swedish Comprehensive school system:

These schools will be of varied types and provide two-year courses in social and technical subjects as well as economics.

Pupils need not go directly from the lower institution to continuation school but may apply for admission after an interval of employment, thus establishing these institutions for flexible age groups of younger and older citizens who wish to improve their education.

AGE OF STUDENT	THE SCHOOL SYSTEM IN SWEDEN										GRADE		
	THEORETICAL STUDIES	SOCIAL STUDIES				TECHNICAL-VOCATIONAL STUDIES		ECONOMIC STUDIES					HIGHER STUDIES
		Humanities	Social Economics	General Practical	Domestic Science	Technical	Practical Vocational	Mercantile	Commercial				
17 – 18	Preparation For Higher Education										12		
16 – 17											11		
15 – 16											10		
14 – 15										RETARDED CHILDREN (NON-GRADED)	9	Upper Department	COMPULSORY EDUCATION
13 – 14	E L E M E N T A R Y S C H O O L					Many course options available.					8		
12 – 13	E L E M E N T A R Y S C H O O L					Few course options available.					7		
11 – 12	E L E M E N T A R Y S C H O O L					No options.					6	Middle Department	
10 – 11	E L E M E N T A R Y S C H O O L					No options.					5		
9 – 10	E L E M E N T A R Y S C H O O L					No options.					4		
8 – 9	E L E M E N T A R Y S C H O O L					No options.					3	Lower Department	
7 – 8	E L E M E N T A R Y S C H O O L					No options.					2		
6 – 7	E L E M E N T A R Y S C H O O L					No options.					1		

YRKESSKOLA
A central School for Domestic Sciences
Stockholm, Sweden

One of the finest unions of good architectural design and well organized educational planning found on this entire survey is embodied in this project.

The site was indeed small for the massive educational program required, and yet the architects refused to sacrifice the valuable ground area needed for richly patterned terraces, landscaped court-yards, and open gardens enhanced with sculptural rock formations. The obvious solution was height—ten floors plus ground level lobbies including a rooftop gymnasium with exercise areas. The student population is to be 1000 female pupils from the ages of 14 to approximately 18. In future stages there will be living accommodations for 50 nonresident students drawn from other parts of Sweden and Europe. The kitchen and dining facilities are designed to prepare and serve 2000 meals per day. In addition, a small day nursery capable of handling 60 youngsters is provided for the convenience of neighboring mothers as well as to provide an opportunity for the students to gain valuable experience in child care. A kindergarten for 30 children is staffed by the older students. Parking for 50 automobiles is provided under the building.

The integrity of the architecture speaks for itself and is a rare accomplishment considering the demanding priority of practical considerations. The design is very powerful with rough textured concrete surfacing contrasted with natural grained wood. The structural system is of exposed concrete with precast concrete aggregate window panels providing the controlled exterior textures. Panels were erected complete with glazing and sealants.

This facility, completed in 1960 and containing 30,000 cubic meters of area, is not yet finished. Still planned are an assembly hall for 350 people, additional administrative offices, and student dormitories.

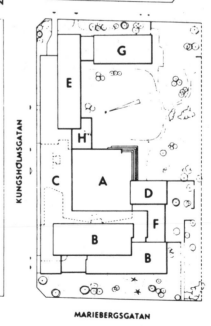

Site Plan
A. School Yard
B. Trade Schools
C. Courses for Adults
D. Assembly Room
E. Consultants' Bureau and
   Central Administration
F. Day Nursery for Infants
G. Students' Living Quarters
H. "Child-parking" Service
(D. E. and G. are not
yet erected)

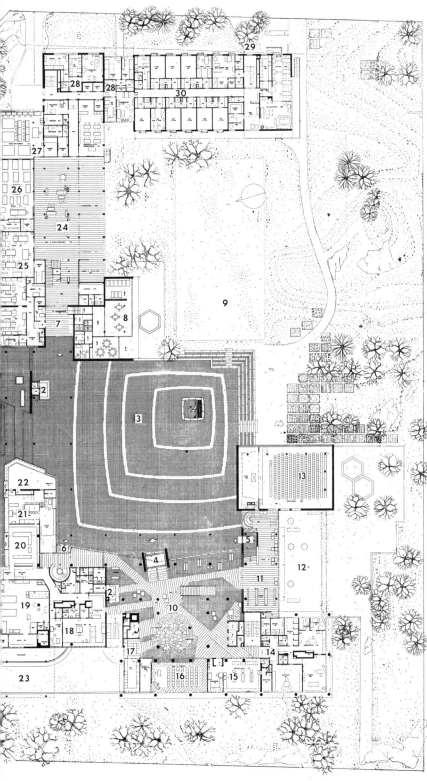

Plan of Ground Floor

1. Main Entrance
2. Caretaker
3. School Yard
4. Entrance to Grade Schools
5. Entrance to Assembly Room
6. Entrance to Part-Time Courses
7. Entrance to Exhibition Rooms, etc.
8. "Child-Parking" Service
9. Playground
10. Hall
11. Foyer and Cloakroom
12. Terrace
13. Assembly Hall
14. Doctor's Reception
15. Grocery Storage and Self-Service Shop
16. Music Room
17. Milk Bar
18. Kitchen where orders for food are taken
19. Bakery
20. Bread and Food Shop
21. Stores Office
22. Hat and Dress Shop
23. Car Ramp
24. Display
25. Needlework Room
26. Weaving Room
27. Bedclothing Courses
28. Apartment
29. Entrance to Students' Living Quarters
30. Students' Living Quarters

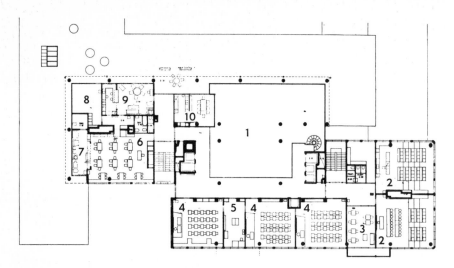

Plan of Second Floor. Scale 1:600. 1. Hall (upper section), 2. Demonstration Laboratory, 3. Smoking and Reading Room, 4. Theory Room, 5. Group Room, 6. Class Room, 7. Laundry, 8. Workshop, 9. Domestic Training Room, 10. Home Kitchen and Students' Dining Room.

Plan of Fourth Floor. Scale 1:600. Domestic Science. 1. Changing Room, 2. Students' Dining Room, 3. School Kitchen, 4. Teacher, 5. Workshop, 6. Domestic Training Room, 7. Students' Hall, 8. Theory Room, 9. Laundry, 10. Needlework Room.

Plan of Seventh Floor. Scale 1:600. Professional Needlework. 1. Changing Room, 2. Tailor, 3. Fitting Room, 4. Storage, 5. Students' Hall, 6. Basic Training, 7. Teacher, 8. Furriers, 9. Fur Sewers.

Plan of Tenth Floor. Scale 1:600. 1. Changing Room, 2. Shower, 3. Drying, 4. Gymnasium, 5. Apparatus, 6. Teacher, 7. Sketching Room, 8. Material, 9. Roof Terrace.

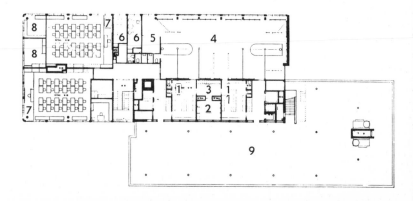

The concept of an entire facility devoted to the "arts of the home" presupposes that girls more inclined to academic pursuits would not matriculate here but would, however, take part time or night courses when they become adults, since every Swedish woman at one time or another is exposed to some domestic training in such a facility. Training rooms with demonstration kitchens are located on the second through the sixth floors, while professional needlework, loom weaving, and fitting rooms occupy the floors above. Each department has its own administrative components. There are, in effect, two distinct schools located "piggyback" fashion in the same building block.

In contrast to the high vertical structure is a low horizontal two story element containing several shops that are outlets for the high quality work produced by the students. A hat and dress shop, crafts and dry goods, and a bakery offer excellent opportunities for retail sales experience as well as a proud commercial outlet for the produce of the school. The high caliber of the goods sold is indicated by the heavy demand for the items displayed. Moreover, it is possible to have items such as rugs, suits, dresses, or even mink coats made to a specified order. The exacting attention given to interior design, under the advisory supervision of the architect, can readily be seen in the fine Scandanavian furniture, fabrics, and lighting fixtures, contributing to a warm homelike atmosphere which cannot help but influence those within toward cultivation of good taste for modern design. The architects were Leonie and Charles Edward Geisendorf, S.I.A.

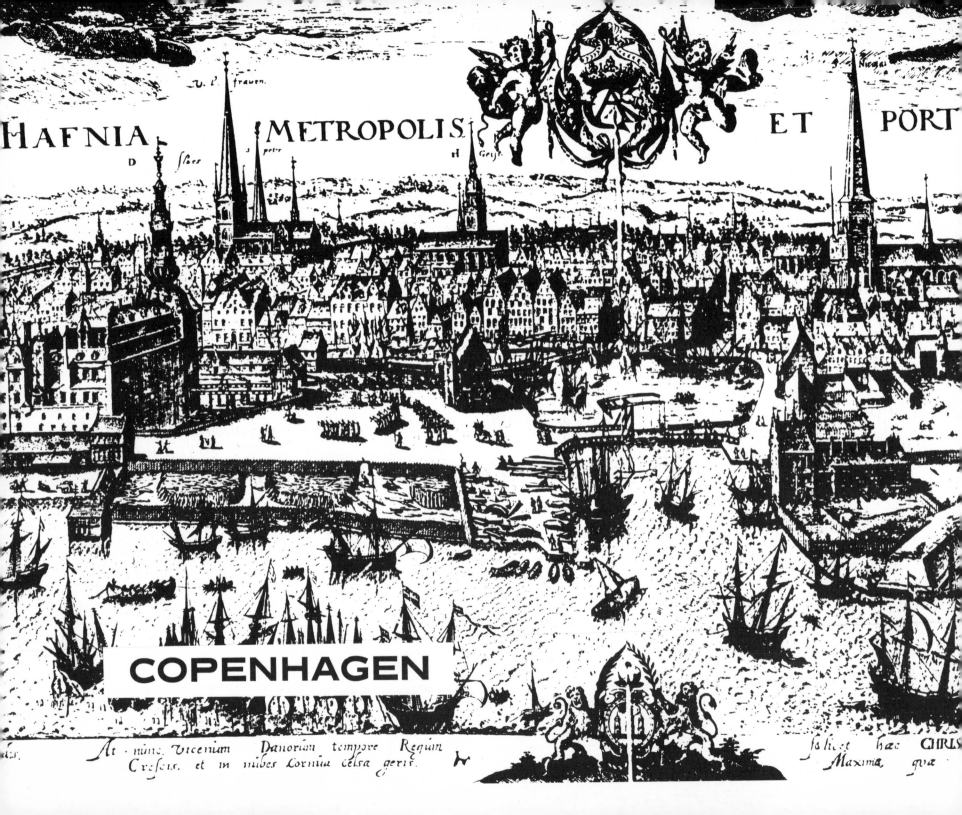

HAFNIA METROPOLIS ET PORT

COPENHAGEN

At nunc Vicenum Danorum tempore Regum
Crescis, et in nubes Cornua celsa geris.

scilicet hæc CHRIS
Maxima, qua

7

COPENHAGEN

The new postwar schools of Copenhagen reveal a definite break with principles that dominated the great school-building period of the 1930's. The large massive school that did not attempt to define the myriad of activities within was then considered the most economic form of building.

This prototype was called the "Aula school" because the several floors of classrooms were grouped around a central hall (aula) which formed the hub of internal traffic as well as serving as an assembly hall.

The modern school with its specialized learning areas demands a more intimate and less monumental approach, and the Danish architects have responded to this need. Their single level structures are frequently built around enclosed school yards to allow various age groups to play separately during recess periods. Whenever possible, school sessions are held in these outdoor surroundings.

One must at this point give the Danish architect credit for what may be his greatest contribution in school planning: interior design within the small scale building concept. His training encompasses all facets of building down to the selection of wallpaper and small appointments and great attention is given the smallest detail.

Perhaps the Danish classic of modern school design is Munkegaard School in Gentofte, Denmark, by Arne Jacobsen. Its checkerboard plan of alternating classroom units and patios makes the structure an outstanding example of the intimacy of a courtyard school. Each section of pavement receives special treatment and the courtyards are embellished by architectural sculpture and landscaping, all carefully selected by architect Jacobsen with characteristic Danish thoroughness.

Approximately one third of the nation's people lives in Copenhagen, whose inhabitants (including suburbs) now number one and a half million. There is a very acute shortage of manpower within the country today, and the strongly organized labor unions carefully restrict the import of foreign tradesmen, which contributes to the difficulty of maintaining construction schedules.

The Copenhagen educational system of today is based on the "Act of February 21, 1961." Municipal authorities make decisions on all matters concerning school finance, curricula, and construction. Administration of schools is the responsibility of the education committee, which consists of the Mayor, an alderman, and four city councillors, with four members elected by the City Council from among the parent-teacher committees of all municipal schools. Each school is in the charge of a headmaster and has a parent-teacher committee of five members.

Each school also has a teacher's council and participates in a joint teachers council for all municipal schools.

The Educational Act of 1958 raised the compulsory educational age to 14; however, 18 is the common age for termination of formal schooling, which begins when the child is 7 years old. Separation of students according to field of study occurs after the fifth year of schooling (age 12) but is not so rigid that crossing "streams" cannot occur. However, unlike Sweden, the streaming of students is based on school administrator's assessment of pupils' daily work and written examinations, although parents' wishes are taken into consideration.

Many schools have recreation centers where children can go after school is over, and educational authorities run various voluntary classes for students. In the summer holiday special activities are arranged for children who stay in the city, while teachers associations see to it that thousands of children spend some time in holiday camps. The teachers associations also run a number of all year round camps that children who would benefit from a longer stay in the country can go to for several months, during which time school sessions are provided.

In 1957 the Ministry of Education in collaboration with the Ministry of Housing issued a collection of school prototypes to be used as a guide for school planning throughout the entire country. This was extensively reviewed and updated in 1961 and revised the entire building program. At that time increased stress was placed upon audio-visual equipment as a teaching aid and "subject-rooms" specifically equipped for their particular use in such subjects as history and languages. Centralized cloakrooms for school bags, books, overcoats, etc., were recommended by this report as a supplement to the classrooms, which would be used for a maximum of thirty hours per week. While such a procedure as "suggested plans" may assure districts of minimum school standards, it was found that these programs must be judiciously supplemented with originality in design innovations and site utilization, lest such rigid requirements as room width (set at 7.5 meters) become inflexible burdens to the architect. The building committee for state gymnasiums uses these prototypes as a basis for its recommendations to the Ministry of Education for approval of building projects (unless there are special local circumstances or particular difficulties in adapting to the building programs of existing schools).

It will be noticed from the following chart that the first several years of school are similar for all students throughout the country, with primary and secondary schooling separated but conducted in the same building.

The use of specialized spaces, such as library, study rooms, and art rooms, is being encouraged for primary students as well as secondary students, the prominent factor in the decision to combine the two groups in one school.

We were informed that most medical care the students may require is given free and, whenever possible, in the medical offices provided in each school. Checkups are given regularly by staff doctors and dentists. The area of psychological treatment is approached objectively and such services are rendered when thought to be required by the student. Nothing sinister is thought of the pupil receiving such assistance. Slow readers account for the majority of those under care, which can run as high as 5 percent of the student body. Parents are always consulted when such remedies are recommended.

All younger children are instructed in swimming once a week, and this is usually held in one of the many municipal pools reserved exclusively for school use in the daytime and converted to adult use in the evening. Some of the newer schools are providing swimming pools on site, and these are shared with neighboring schools.

Much attention is given to landscaping as an integral part of the education process, and buildings are handsomely set off with lawns, planting, trees, pools, and sculpture, all in a very good state of maintenance. Automobile parking is minimal, usually only for teachers and visitors, but students are provided ample and accessible storage for their bicycles. Bomb shelters are apparently provided in all schools, usually for a capacity in excess of the total school population.

Danish character is achieved in their buildings not only by the extensive use of natural materials and the absence of synthetic ones, but also by the scale of the components utilized. Small details such as brick paving for courtyards, birdbaths, benches used liberally over the site, scaled down lighting fixtures, etc., greatly contribute to the child-oriented atmosphere these schools achieve.

AGE OF STUDENT	THE SCHOOL SYSTEM IN DENMARK								SCHOOL GRADE	
		UNIVERSITY (Five Years)								
18 – 19		LANGUAGES			MATHEMATICS				12	GYMNASIUM
17 – 18		Modern Languages	Civics	Classic Languages	Physics Mathematics	Civics	Natural Sciences		11	
16 – 17	VOCATIONAL ←	MIDDLE SCHOOL ("REAL DEPARTMENT")							10	
15 – 16	(3 YEARS PART TIME	MIDDLE SCHOOL ("REAL DEPARTMENT")							9	
14 – 15	OR 1 YEAR FULL TIME)	MIDDLE SCHOOL ("REAL DEPARTMENT")							8	
13 – 14	PRIMARY SCHOOL ("FOLKESKOLEN")							RETARDED CHILDREN (NON-GRADED)	7	COMPULSORY EDUCATION
12 – 13	PRIMARY SCHOOL ("FOLKESKOLEN")								6	
11 – 12	PRIMARY SCHOOL ("FOLKESKOLEN")								5	
10 – 11	PRIMARY SCHOOL ("FOLKESKOLEN")								4	
9 – 10	PRIMARY SCHOOL ("FOLKESKOLEN")								3	
8 – 9	PRIMARY SCHOOL ("FOLKESKOLEN")								2	
7 – 8	PRIMARY SCHOOL ("FOLKESKOLEN")								1	

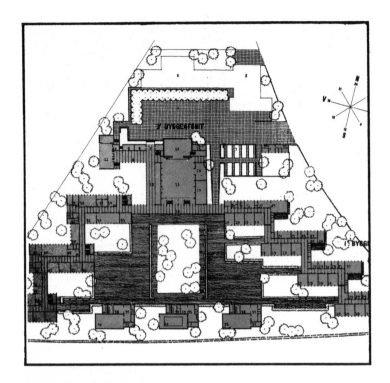

BUDDINGE SKOLE and
GLADSAXE GYMNASIUM
Copenhagen, Denmark

The extent of community participation within the school building program and its ultimate usage of the facilities is very well developed. The community school is usually designed with adult as well as children's needs in mind, and it appears that they achieve a high return on their investment dollar, in terms of total community welfare. An outstanding example of this is the Buddinge Skole for Gladsaxe by the gifted architectural husband and wife team of Eva and Nils Koppel. This community of 70,000 people, with an ultimate planned population of 110,000, invested their own money in the school's athletic facility with one provision: that the building could be utilized for theatrical events, concerts, or public lectures, as well as conventional sports activities. The solution turned out to be ingenious although remarkably uncomplicated. The dead level wood strip floor is carefully designed and, with the assistance of synchronized hydraulic jacks, raises a full ten feet at one end, providing the necessary angle for unobstructed auditorium viewing. Chairs can be fixed to inserts in the floor, and special detailing of retractable plates around the two story columns allows the free movement of the floor around the structure. Locker rooms as well as theatrical dressing rooms are provided in the lower level, and the large, fully commercial stage is ample for even the most ambitious television production or symphonic presentation.

Gladsaxe has three large swimming pools serving the community which are used for school students in the daytime and adults in the evening.

The Gladsaxe community "shared" school facility is not unique in Denmark, and we encountered several of these student-public auditorium facilities in Copenhagen, although Gladsaxe was the only one with the "tilt-up" floor system.

Commercial cloak checking areas are provided on each side of the main auditorium as well as rest rooms, snack bars, and lobby. This entire space can be independently utilized in day or evening since all circulation has been designed not to interfere with school usage.

Conversely, maximum security of the school is maintained when only the auditorium is being utilized. A wise investment for this expanding suburb of Copenhagen, growing at the rate of 10,000 apartments per year.

Since evening school is very popular in Denmark, a leader in adult evening education since 1897, many community schools hardly ever close but carry full adult educational loads as well. These are free except for small administrative and material supply charges. Frequently, school libraries double as community libraries with evening hours reserved for adult usage.

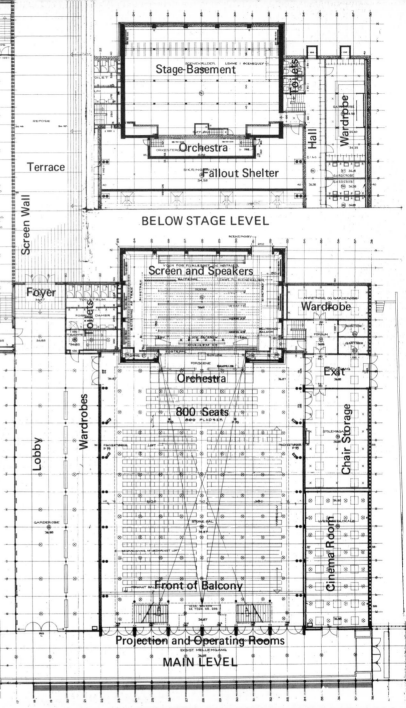

Stage-Basement

Toilets

Hall

Wardrobe

Terrace

Orchestra

Fallout Shelter

Screen Wall

BELOW STAGE LEVEL

Screen and Speakers

Foyer

Toilets

Wardrobe

Orchestra

Exit

Lobby

Wardrobes

800 Seats

Chair Storage

Cinema Room

Front of Balcony

Projection and Operating Rooms

MAIN LEVEL

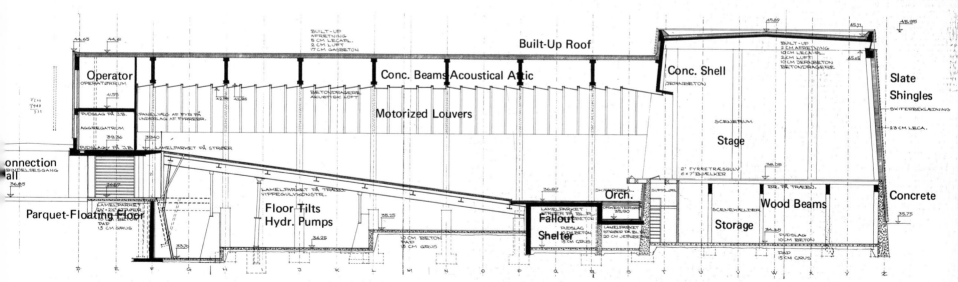

BUILT-UP
AFRETNING
5 CM LECABL.
2 CM LUFT
17 CM GASBETON

Built-Up Roof

BUILT-UP
2 CM AFRETNING
10CM LECA-BL.
2CM LUFT
10 CM JERNBETON
BETONDRAGERE

44.65   44.61   45.89   45.71   45.95

Operator   **Conc. Beams** **Acoustical Attic**   **Conc. Shell**   45.65

OPERATØRRUM   JERNBETON   **Slate**
4155   **Shingles**

BETONDRAGERE
AKUSTISK LOFT   SKIFERBEKLÆDNING

PUDSLAG PÅ J.B.   PANELVÆG AF FYR PÅ   **Motorized Louvers**   SCENERUM   23 CM LECA.
                      UNDERLAG AF FYRREBR.
AGGREGATRUM 39.36   **Stage**
             3940

PUDSLAG PÅ J.B.   LAMELPARKET PÅ STRØER   36.05

onnection   2' FYRRETRÆSGULV
all   6×7' BJÆLKER   **Concrete**
BINDELSESGANG   SKIFERBESKL.
36.85
                  LAMELPARKET PÅ TRÆBJ.   36.97   BJÆLKER PÅ TRÆBJ.
                  VIPPEGULVKONSTR.   35.75
Parquet-Floating Floor   LAMELPARKET   **Floor Tilts**   **Fallout** **Orch.** **Wood Beams**
             4×1' 2×2' STRØER   **Hydr. Pumps**   **Shelter** ORCESTERGRAV SCENEKÆLDER
             PAD   35.25   LAMELPARKET   35.90   **Storage**   34.65
             15 CM GRUS 33.75   STRØER PÅ BL. PL.   PUDSLAG
                                             34.25   PUDSLAG   10CM BETON
                                                          0 CM BETON 15 CM GRUS LAMELPARKET   PAD
                                                          PAD   STRØER PÅ BL. BL.   15 CM GRUS
                                                          15 CM GRUS   20 CM JERNBETON

CREDITS

LONDON

School	Architect	Photographer
Acland Burghley	Howell, Killick, Partridge and Amis Chartered Architects	John Donat
Beaufoy	The Architects Co-Partnership, C.A.	The Architects Co-Partnership
Tudor	Scherrer & Hicks, C.A.	Sidney W. Newbery
Sarah Siddons	London County Council School construction div.	London County Council Authors
Battersea Park	Hubert Bennett, F.R.I.B.A.	Authors
Barn Elms School Sports Center	London County Council School construction div.	London County Council

ZURICH

Hauswirtschaftliche Fortbildungsschule	Ernst Schindler Dipl. Architekt. B.S.A., S.I.A.	Photo of model by Architect
Kantonsschule Freudenberg	Prof. J. Schader Architect B.S.A./S.I.A.	Kunstgewerbeschule Zurich
Riedhof	Prof. Alfred Roth Architect B.S.A./S.I.A.	Walter Binder

HAMBURG

School	Architect	Photographer
Altona Königstrasse	Paul Seitz Dipl. Architect	Authors
Sülldorfer Kirchenweg	Buildings: Hamburg Schulbehörde Landscape: Hamburg Schulbehörde garden dept.	Staatliche Landesbildstelle, Hamburg
Golbach Valley	Buildings: Hamburg Schulbehörde Landscape: Hamburg Schulbehörde garden dept.	Staatliche Landesbildstelle, Hamburg

STOCKHOLM

Yrkesskola	Leonie and Charles-Edward Geisendorf, Architects S.I.A.	Ateljé Sundahl, Jonathan King, and Authors

COPENHAGEN

Gladsaxe Gymnasium, Buddinge Skole	Eva and Nils Koppel Arkitekter, M.A.A.	Authors

AUTHORS BIOGRAPHICAL SKETCHES

John W. McLeod, F.A.I.A.

A principal in the firm of McLeod, Ferrara and Ensign, of Washington, D.C., Mr. McLeod was former chairman of the A.I.A. National Committee of school and college buildings, and his firm has designed several hundred school and college buildings in the United States and abroad. He has twice served as a member of the U.S. Delegation to UNESCO International Conferences on school building programs in Switzerland and England.

Mr. McLeod has served as a member of a joint national committee which recently published the new "Guide for School Lighting," and was also a member of AASA's editorial board for the publication of the book "Planning America's Schools." He recently was co-author of a book on mathematical facilities, published by Columbia University Press, and is a frequent speaker and participant at school building conferences and conventions.

Richard J. Passantino, A.I.A.

Mr. Passantino received his architectural degree from the University of Cincinnati in 1957, with postgraduate work at The American University from 1958 to 1959. He was planning officer for three years at Bolling Air Force Base, Washington, D.C., before joining the firm of McLeod, Ferrara and Ensign in 1961 to assist in the planning of the Haile Selassie I University in Addis Ababa, Ethiopia. Recently he has been made research associate for the firm and has coordinated two previous E.F.L. releases: the publication "Building and Facilities for the Mathematical Sciences," of which Mr. McLeod was co-author, and the film on geodesic fieldhouse construction, "Exercise in Economy."